BLOGGIN' BASEBALL II

(from the bleachers)

Copyright © 2015 Andrew Wolfenson

ISBN-13:   978-0692583456

ISBN-10:   0692583459

Balding Legal Publishing

2414 Morris Avenue, Suite 104, Union, NJ 07083

FOREWARD

Once upon a time, there was a blogging site on the internet known as "Open Salon". For six years, I posted various musings on the site, whenever the urge arose, and continued to do so until the site was unceremoniously shut down by its parent company. The blog posts themselves, therefore, do not currently exist in their original forms, such that they cannot be located by searching the internet. That does not mean, however, that the contents of such posts are also extinct.

Three years ago, I published *Bloggin' Baseball (from the bench)*, a collection of such blogs with updated information and commentary. The posts contained in that book, therefore, live on in print. For the ones posted after its publication, however, no such permanency existed.

Until now, that is. Contained within this book, the follow-up to the original *Bloggin' Baseball*, are the baseball-related posts which were written after the previous book was released. I have also included some posts about other sports, those posts which touched not only on the world of sports, but on society in general. Like in the first book, I have endeavored to provide updated information as to most of the posts, to make the content of this book more topical than a mere re-publication of the original posts. It is my opinion that several continue to stand on their own, however, and that additional commentary would be superfluous. For those posts, no such commentary is included.

As I stated in the foreword to the first book, you may disagree with some of the points, or even many of the points, expressed herein. It remains the beauty of sport, however, that we can agree to disagree. At the very least, I hope that the content of this book causes you to think, and maybe change your opinion on a topic or two. That, of course, is the ultimate compliment to any writer.

In fact, pause after you read the post about Jim Valvano. If you have done all three of the things that Valvano said you should do each day, while reading these pages, then I have unquestionably accomplished my goal in publishing the book.

ACKNOWLEDGEMENTS

I wish to thank Diana Ani Stokely for her revised version of the "Bloggin' Baseball" cover, the fifth book cover that she has created for me over the past few years. I could not imagine contacting anyone else to work with me on the cover art. I also want to thank, for the second time, my friend and former F&M classmate Brian Lewbart, whose almost 30-year old photo of a certain newspaper editor has gained new life as the cover art for this and the prior "Bloggin' Baseball" book.

I also want to thank those who wrote with me on the pages of Open Salon, especially those who took the time to read my posts, comment (even if not favorably) and who forced me to bring my "A game" every time I wandered into their midst – in alphabetical order – Amy Abbott, Gerald Andersen, Dale Anderson, Heidi Banerjee, Bill Beck, Lezlie Bishop, John Blumenthal, Richard Brown, Joan Haskins, Lea Lane, Nick Leshi, David McClain, Matt Paust, Alysa Salzburg, Andy Schulkind, Lisa Schnaidt, Linda Seccaspina, Rita Shibr, Adam Sifre, Sally Swift, and Jonathan Wolfman. I want to also extend thanks to those who wrote under nom de plumes, such as Abrawang, AtHomePilgrim, Connie Mack, Dr. Spudman, and Koshersalaami. Posthumously, I honor and remember Kenny Sibbett, a fellow Yankee fan and friend whose quote graces the front cover of this book. Any omissions from this list are accidental.

Of course, I need to include my parents, siblings, and other family members. Special mention to my father, father-in-law, and uncle, the trio from the prior generation with whom I can spend hours chatting about sports – and which is never wasted time.

Next, special thanks to my children, Sara, Danielle, Alina, and DJ Wolfenson, who are joined this time by their little brother, Cooper.

Lastly, even more special thanks my wife, Jennifer. Again, she has graciously granted me the time to disappear into my den to write this book, although I suspect that she secretly likes not having me around. After 26 years of being married to me, it would not be hard to blame her.

For my wife, Jennifer, who agreed that each of my daughters should come home from the hospital in a Yankee outfit

TABLE OF CONTENTS

CHAPTER 1 – YANKEES AND METS

(two teams trying to take a larger bite of the Big Apple)

METS SWEEP YANKEES!! A MUSICAL SALUTE TO THE VICTORS

(Originally posted May 31, 2013)

Last night, the Mets completed a four-game sweep of the previously-mighty Yankees. This is the first time that the Mets have taken every game from the Bronx Bombers in a season, and the Mets' faithful are, properly, sticking it to Yankee Nation.

In reality, losing four games to the Mets is not an apocalyptic event for the Yankees - but when one looks at how the Mets exposed the Yankees' weaknesses, their inability to score runs and their thin starting pitching staff, concerns must arise. The Yankees simply are not a first-place team, despite the surprising success that they had enjoyed until they ran into the juggernaut from Citifield.

I have, in the past, taken great pains to bash the Mets and their ineptitude. Now, in light of their destruction of my Yankees, I present the following homage to the Mets - perhaps appropriately, to the tune of Queen's epic "We will Rock You/We are the Champions" - congratulations to the Mets and their fans - may this sweep be the start of great things for your young nucleus, so that New York has at least one competitive team moving forward.

METS:

Yankees always crowing, making big noise, playing in the Bronx think they own New York all day

Now they got egg on their face, they're a big disgrace, we kicked their butts all over the place

We just we just swept you!   All four games, we just swept you!

13

BLOGGIN' BASEBALL II (FROM THE BLEACHERS) - ANDREW WOLFENSON

Yankees you're a bunch of old men, come back to Queens we'll beat you again today

Kicked you right in the face, even in your place, 27 banners don't mean nothing, should just put them away

We just we just swept you!   The Mets! Yes, we just swept you!

Yankees think you're so good, big men, pleadin' to fans it don't matter you'll beat up the Sox today

But you can't look us in the eye, dominated you can't deny, today we're kings of Big Apple, not just a bunch of young guys

We just we just swept you!   We just we just swept you!

YANKEES:

We've won it all, more than two dozen times, now we have to admit, that we're way past our primes

Old brittle bones? We've got more than a few, being swept by the Mets is so bad, so sad, we thought we couldn't lose

We were once Champions, my friends. But now we must realize, our time at the top is at end

We were once Champions, we were once Champions. Now getting swept by the Mets it's clear we're just losers

But we were once Champions, of the world

We used to take bows, all those Bronx curtain calls, George and Hal paid us a king's fortune & we enjoyed all of it

27 times we won it all

But now we're aging millionaires, being in first place was just a ruse, we faced a challenge this week and we failed, four times did we lose

We were once Champions, my friends. Swept by a Triple A team? Clearly our time on top is at end

We were once Champions, we were once Champions. Don't score any runs and can't rely on our starting pitchers

Hard to believe that we were once Champions, of the world

Extra Innings: This sweep was just another step in the Mets' ascension to their status as the better New York baseball team. The youth movement in Queens finally took hold in 2015, as a quartet of young pitchers led the Mets to the World Series, where they were defeated in five games by the Kansas City Royals. Despite the loss, the Mets' faithful had to be encouraged at their future, a future riding on the golden wings of hurlers Matt Harvey, Jason deGrom, Noah Syndergaard, and Steven Matz.

Across town, the Yankees did manage to slide into the playoffs, carried for half a season by Alex Rodriguez; A-Rod, fresh off a suspension which sidelined him for the entire 2014 season, carried the team through the All-Star game; in the second half of the season, Rodriguez, along with the team's other aging veterans, performed at a much lower level and the Yankees were forced to settle for a Wild Card game. The day before the game, the team was shocked when veteran pitcher CC Sabathia announced that he was entering a rehab center for alcohol addiction. The team then went out and, despite Rodriguez's proclamation that "we play for CC", managed but three hits off of Houston ace Dallas Keuchel and were sent packing for the winter – a winter that will likely last several seasons, as the team remains shackled by large contracts to aging veterans.

What Do JDate and the Yankees Have in Common?

(Originally posted July 10, 2013)

The answer, of course, is singles.

The New York Yankees were once known as *"Murderer's Row"* in the 1920's, a team which boasted two of the greatest sluggers in baseball history, Babe Ruth and Lou Gehrig. In the 1960's, the team featured a new generation of power hitters, the slugging tandem of Roger Maris and Mickey Mantle. Today, however, the team is comprised largely of "Punch and Judy" hitters, batsmen who can barely force a ball past the infield and who populate their statistics with little more than singles.

JDate, meanwhile, boasts that it is the internet's premier dating site for eligible Jewish singles. According to the site, it is now home to 9,457 such singles, each of whom is searching for their "Member of the Tribe" soul mate. The site boasts that tens of thousands of singles interact via its site each day, likely more people than who pass through the Yankee Stadium turnstiles on any given day to watch the faux-Yankees take the field. The announced attendances at the games are just that – announced figures – simply looking around the empty seats throughout the Stadium belies the fact that the numbers are grossly inflated.

As for the team itself, the numbers are stark. Over the past four days, the Yankees have been only 9,427 singles short of JDate, as their hit totals from Saturday through today were, in order, 10, 6, 9, and 6. With the exception of a pinch-hit home run from Lyle Overbay, all of these hits were, you guessed it, singles.

Granted, the Yankees are playing without their presumed trio of All-Star sluggers, Curtis Granderson, Mark Teixeira, and Alex Rodriguez. These three, along with Captain Derek Jeter, have spent all or most of this season on the Disabled List while pocketing their combined almost $100,000,000 in salaries. While those four have been home or rehabilitating their injuries, the Yankee roster is populated by such non-stars as Chris Stewart, Austin Romine, Luis Cruz, Jayson Nix, Alberto Gonzalez, Travis Ishakawa, Eduardo Nunez, and Zoilo Almonte. There are holdover players such as Ichiro Suzuki and Brett Gardner, but those two have essentially made their careers stroking, that's right, singles.

Last Saturday, the Yankees strung together their singles sufficiently to score some runs, and escaped with a victory over Baltimore. Sunday, however, their collection of one-base hits led to only one run, and the (allegedly) 40,000 fans who braved oppressive heat to cheer for the home team (this writer included) went home saddened when closer extraordinaire Mariano Rivera wilted in the Bronx sauna and gave up a game-losing home run (that's an extra-base hit, for the unindoctrinated) to the Orioles' Adam Jones. Monday and Tuesday brought more offensive futility, with a total of 14 singles wrapped around Overbay's solitary blast – the team only plated one run in each of the two games, losing both to the Kansas City Royals. That's three runs in three games, and only one hit that resulted in the batter moving past first base.

Just for basis of comparison, the White Sox' Alex Rios tallied six hits all by his lonesome last night. Five of those knocks were singles, and he added a triple just to differentiate himself from the Yankees' lineup.

Things have gotten so bad in the Bronx that fans and pundits are *actually looking forward* to the possible return of that other Alex, Alex Rodriguez. At the beginning of the season, when news broke of new steroid allegations against A-Roid, fans and writers alike were united in their call for the Yankees to seek to void his contract, and looked forward to the possibility of never seeing him don the home pinstripes again. Now, however, the Yankee faithful have watched third

18

base be manned in his absence by a broken and battered Kevin Youkilis, a hitless wonder known by the moniker David Adams (at one point he was hitless in 32 at-bats), and others such as the afore-mentioned Nix and Gonzalez. These men have tried, in vain, to muster even a modicum of production from their position at third base; their failure to do so, however, has rendered the "hot corner" a "tepid pitstop" at best. The common consensus now is that A-Rod can do no worse than this parade of replacements; at the very least, even an un-steroid fueled Alex Rodriguez is still capable of stroking an occasional double or even, gasp, a home run.

*****

Baseball's rumor mill is again abuzz, however, with predictions of a suspension for A-Rod. He is apparently one of the players who will be meeting with Major League Baseball to talk about his connection, if any, with Biogenesis. Other players, most notably former MVP Ryan Braun, reportedly have refused to speak to the sport's top brass. If the reports are correct, then it is possible that A-Rod will be suspended perhaps for the majority or all of the remainder of the 2013 season.

On another side note, Kevin Youkilis is Jewish, but he is no longer eligible for dating sites as he married Tom Brady's sister last year, spurning the urge to enroll on JDate and marry someone from his own religion. Also, the likelihood is that he will never again play for the Yankees, so the slot reserved for "Yankee Jew" is now open – maybe they can get Ike Davis from the Mets – Davis is the perfect ballplayer – half a Yankee (his dad is former Yankees' reliever Ron Davis) and half a Jew (his mom is Jewish).

*****

On JDate, it should be noted, one can browse for free and then, presumably, there is a sign-up fee so that singles can actually meet other singles. No doubt, however, the sign-up fees are less than the exorbitant ticket prices that

19

the Yankees demand for lower-level seats in the Stadium, where fans can see the players' singles. In the Stadium, however, it is rare that the singles appear in such bunches to allow for a run to score – unless, of course, it is for the other team.

Next month marks my 24th wedding anniversary. If I do not do anything completely stupid, then I will have no need for JDate or the 9,457 singles currently populating its site, at least for the foreseeable future. At the same time, if the pretend "baby bombers" do not start hitting like their formidable predecessors, then I will similarly have no need for the multitude of singles which will populate the daily box scores.

Someone should remind the Yankees' hitters that football season starts in only two months. If they continue their recent power outage, then they, like the fans, will be sitting home and watching football come October.

Extra Innings: In 2015, the team finished second in the major leagues in runs scored and fourth in home runs. As they were led by aging veterans Alex Rodriguez and Mark Teixeira, how much power the team will have in 2016 and beyond is speculative at best.

Proof That G-D Simply Isn't a Mets' Fan

(Originally posted August 26, 2013)

Today we were provided with clear, convincing proof that G-d is not a Mets' fan. He simply can't be.

That, or maybe the Devil, to the extent that he really exists, actually runs Major League Baseball.

Whoever is calling the shots, whether Beelzebub or someone else, is being very, very cruel to the fans of the team from Queens. Sure, the Mets have been given gifts in the past - the '69 team was even called the "Miracle Mets" - and the '86 World Series would not have been won if not for some divine intervention on a slow-rolling ball that somehow found its way through a gimp's legs. But other than those two occasions, this franchise has been, in a word, snake-bitten. Every time they seem to be on the verge of something positive, disaster strikes.

Maybe using the word "disaster" is a bit extreme - but if you are a Mets' fan, the news today about Matt Harvey really must feel like Armageddon. Harvey is the crown jewel of the Mets' pitching staff, the first rookie pitcher to start an All-Star game since Mark "the Bird" Fidrych in 1976. With Harvey on the mound, Mets' fans had reason to believe that the team's future was filled with promise - a pitching staff anchored by Harvey and which also included youngsters Zack Wheeler, Jon Niese, and Dillon Gee could compare, in a couple of years, with any rotation in the league. Snapping up a couple more hitters to complement third baseman David Wright would ensure competitiveness, if not more, from the Mets.

Many Yankees' fans (this writer included) also believed that the Mets would be running the Big Apple within the next couple of years, as the aging,

21

heavy-contract-laden Bronx Bombers would no doubt languish while the young, upstart Mets would take the league by storm.

Sadly, faster than you could invoke the names Pulsipher, Wilson, and Isringhausen (the last time the Mets had a young nucleus of pitchers which imploded) it has all come crashing down. Today came word that Matt Harvey, the crown jewel, has a torn ligament in his elbow and may require "Tommy John" surgery, which would sideline him for the entire 2014 season, if not longer. Gone are the hopes of a pitching dynasty. Gone are the hopes that the team could be competitive in 2014.

For some, gone are the hopes that this team would ever again have a chance at greatness.

It is impossible not to pity the Mets' fan at this point. Harvey, and the promise of his future greatness, had provided the fan base with its best hopes of success since youthful, pre-drug abusing Dwight Gooden and Darryl Strawberry donned the blue and orange uniforms. One cannot blame the Mets' fan for asking "why us? Why now" a la Nancy Kerrigan.

Perhaps it is simply not the Mets' time. But if recent history is any indicator, it may never again be the Mets' time. And don't even get me started on the football team that used to share Shea Stadium with the Mets. Aside from their own miracle in 1969, no team has been as snake-bitten as the New York Jets. Just ask Mark Sanchez.

Extra Innings: To a large extent, the Mets exorcised their demons and returned to meaningful October baseball in 2015, even tasting November baseball for the first time as they reached the World Series before succumbing to Kansas City in five games. For those who still want to believe that the Mets are somehow cursed, however, the Series did provide some poetic moments to consider.

A victory in Game 4 was critical; that game was lost, however, in large part due to an error committed by Daniel Murphy, who up until that point had been the team's star of the post-season. Murphy had homered in six consecutive post-season games, setting a team record, so his error was a crushing blow to his prior success. A base-running mistake in that same game was also quite costly – a mistake committed by Yoenis Cespedes, the man whose mid-season acquisition unquestionably turned the team's season around. Cespedes slugged 17 home runs in his first month as a Met, and set the team on a course where it gained command of the National League Eastern Division, a lead which they never relinquished.

Lastly, there was Matt Harvey, the team's ace hurler. The man known as the "Dark Knight" pitched eight stellar innings in Game 5, an elimination game for the team, and the Mets went into the 9th inning on the positive side of a 2-0 score. Harvey talked manager Terry Collins into allowing him to pitch the final inning, and Harvey's hubris proved detrimental to the team as Kansas City scored two runs in the frame, tying the score and putting the contest into extra innings. Sometime later, the Royals tallied five additional runs and captured the championship by a 7-2 score.

BLOGGIN' BASEBALL II (FROM THE BLEACHERS) - ANDREW WOLFENSON

Saying Goodbye to Mariano Rivera - An Emotional Bronx Weekend

(Originally posted September 23, 2013)

This past weekend was an extremely bittersweet one for Yankees' fans. It was a weekend full of emotion, not all positive, and a weekend in which the team, facing elimination from the post-season picture, showed signs of life and the heart, the desire, to remain in the hunt for another trip to October play. It was a weekend of hope, of false promises, and of remembering the achievements of two of the team's biggest contributors while also witnessing a sneak preview of the struggles that will face this team in years to come.

<u>Friday night</u>

The emotional roller-coaster, at least for baseball purists, began during Friday night's game. The Yankees ace, CC Sabathia, pitched to his capabilities for the first time in months and out-dueled another former Cy Young Award winner, the Giants' Tim Lincecum, en route to a 5-1 Yankees victory in a game that the team desperately needed to win in order to keep pace with the other playoff contenders.

The key to this game, however, was the go-ahead hit, a seventh-inning home run by the much-maligned Alex Rodriguez. This was just not any home run, however – it was a grand slam, and snapped a 1-1 tie, putting the Yanks ahead 5-1 with a lead that they would never relinquish. And it was also not just any grand slam, either – the blast gave A-Rod 24 grand slams for his career, making him baseball's all-time leader for such homers – and breaking a tie with Yankee great Lou Gehrig, who had held the record with 23 since his retirement in 1939.

But did Yankee fans appreciate A-Rod taking the grand slam crown from Gehrig? Reaction from the crowd at the ballpark seemed mixed. In my home, however, the reaction was clearly not positive for Rodriguez. At the risk of plagiarizing myself, here is the post that I put on Facebook immediately after Rodriguez touched home plate:

> *It's a bittersweet evening in Yankee nation - Alex Rodriguez just hit a grand slam to put the Yanks ahead in a game they must win - but the blast was the 24th of his career, moving him ahead of all-time Yankee great Lou Gehrig and which makes A-Rod the sole owner of the career grand slam record. By all accounts, the quiet, honorable Gehrig was the exact opposite of A-Rod - he sought to avoid the spotlight, not live within its glare; he was the consummate teammate, not the "me first" player that A-Rod has come to personify; he played in 2,130 consecutive games without synthetic or medicinal assistance, whereas A–Rod, of course, has used steroids. To me, Lou Gehrig is, was, and will be the career grand slam leader with a pure number of 23, not A-Rod's tainted 24.*

Yankee announcer Michael Kay also explored the mixed emotions of the evening during that evening's YES broadcast. Yet again, the specter of Rodriguez's steroid use, the threat of suspension hanging over his head, and his continued refusal to admit to any of the allegations against him continued to work against Alex. So while the victory was celebrated in the television booth and at the Wolfenson home in NJ, the blast that directly led to the win was not given the historical statute that would have been provided had the record been broken by a "clean" player.

<u>Sunday afternoon</u>

Sunday's game had all of the makings of an emotional outpouring once it was announced that the Yankees would be honoring their closer, Mariano Rivera, prior to the game. Rivera is, without question, the greatest closer in baseball history. There is no need to recount his statistics here (links to prior posts about Mariano are below). He is also hailed as one of the nicest people in the game, and one cannot overstate the respect that the remainder of the league has for Rivera. After announcing that this would be his last season, the major league's all-time leader in saves has been feted at numerous ballparks, been given gifts from teams across the American League, and was honored at this season's All-Star game. Clearly the home celebration, however, would be best.

The anticipation was also punctuated by rumor and a later announcement. Since being installed as the Yankees' closer in 1997, Rivera has jogged to the mound from the bullpen to the sounds of Metallica's classic, "*Enter Sandman*." The band was scheduled to play an invitation-only concert at Harlem's Apollo Theater the night before, so rumors began circulating that they would appear at the Sunday afternoon game to play the song live. Also, one of the fellow members of the Yankees' iconic "Core Four," left-hander Andy Pettitte, announced earlier in the week that he would also be retiring at season's end. His last start in Yankee Stadium would be on Sunday.

This is Pettitte's second go-round at retirement. When he retired the first time, I penned a blog about the inevitable end of the Yankee dynasty due to the aging and retirements of the Yankee veterans, and posited that his statistics were not stellar enough for him to earn a future place alongside Rivera in baseball's Hall of Fame. The link for that post is also below, and my opinion has not changed. Pettitte retires with 255 regular-season victories and, more importantly to some, a record 19 victories in post-season play. But just like two years ago, these numbers are simply not Hall of Fame caliber.

Pettitte received a great deal of love from the capacity crowd as he took the mound for the game, but the day truly belonged, as it should, to Mariano.

*****

BLOGGIN' BASEBALL II (FROM THE BLEACHERS) - ANDREW WOLFENSON

On a personal note, I had the privilege of attending Sunday's Mariano farewell with two men who have been a large part of feeding my love for baseball and the Yankees – my father and my father-in-law. It was my dad who first introduced me to baseball, and, over the years, would regale me with tales of the old Brooklyn Dodgers, the fights between the members of New York's different boroughs over which team was better, and the heartbreak in Brooklyn when the team moved to Los Angeles. As I got older, he would send me clippings from the local newspapers to keep me abreast of baseball goings-on while I was in places that did not have proper media coverage, like summer camp and Lancaster, PA (pre-internet, of course). My father-in-law has had Yankees' season tickets for decades, and has been kind enough to provide me with tickets to dozens of games over the past 25 years. He also instilled a love for the Yankees in his eldest daughter, which has made my life quite easy at times, especially when I wanted my daughters to come home from the hospital for the first time in a Yankee outfit.

My dad and I before the game

The Yankees pulled out all of the stops for Mariano on his special day. The "ceremony" began with Rachel Robinson and Mariano unveiling a new plaque in the Stadium's Monument Park for her late husband, the great Jackie Robinson. Mariano is the last major league player to wear number 42, which was retired across the entire major leagues in Robinson's honor some years ago – only those then wearing the number could continue to do so, and Mariano is the last of those players – Mariano then unveiled his own pinstriped #42 in Monument Park, joined by his wife and three sons.

A cast of luminaries was then announced to the crowd, including former teammates David Cone, Hideki Matsui, Tino Martinez, Paul O'Neill, and Bernie Williams. Former manager Joe Torre was also in attendance, as was former Yankee GM Gene Michael, architect of the five-time World Series champion dynasty. The loudest ovations, standing ovations, were given to former fan favorites Matsui, Martinez and Williams. Rivera was introduced, and he walked to the mound from the bullpen to the familiar strains of "*Enter Sandman.*" This time, however, the song was not the recorded version. Rather, the band itself was playing in center field, as had been rumored. Rivera's slow walk to the mound and his turning to the crowd in several directions while tipping his cap after he reached it, were met by sustained cheers and chants of "Mar-i-a-no!"

Metallica belting out Mariano's signature song - "Enter Sandman"

Various presents were given to Mariano, including two from the visiting Giants - a painting depicting Mariano pitching in their home stadium of AT&T Park and a guitar designed by Kirk Hammett of Metallica and signed by baseball legend Willie Mays. The band also presented a gift, a speaker emblazoned with the "Enter Sandman" name and Rivera's number 42. Lastly, the team provided its gifts, including a rocking chair made of baseball bats, a $100,000 check to his foundation, a framed version of his Monument Park plaque and number, and a Waterford crystal depiction of his glove.

True Yankee fans also noted, no doubt, two other "historical" details – first, a video honoring Rivera included the unmistakable voice of the late Bob Sheppard – *"now coming in to pitch, number 42, Mariano Rivera, number 42"* – and the National Anthem was sung, via recording, by another former "voice" of the Yankees, the late Robert Merrill.

Given the chance to speak to the crowd, Rivera was his usual humble self, thanking G-d for the ability to play, and, to laughter, thanking his parents for "having" him. He thanked all of his teammates, the Yankee organization, and both his home country of Panama and his adopted country of America. And when it was time to finish, he again thanked everyone, including the fans, and said that it was time to play ball.

Had this been a Hollywood movie, Andy Pettitte would have pitched a fantastic game, the offense would have scored some runs, and Mariano would have come in for the save, to preserve Pettitte's victory in his final home start. But this game was in the Bronx, and not in Hollywood. Pettitte did his best, actually pitching a no-hitter for five innings before giving up a home run (to SF shortstop Ehire Adrianza, the first home run in his career) in the sixth inning. Unfortunately for the Yankees, their offense wasn't much better against the Giants' pitcher (interestingly, named Yusmeiro "Petit") and they were only able to put up one run in the first six innings. In the seventh inning, Pettitte threw his 100th pitch of the game and it was clear that it was time for him to leave the game. Manager Joe

Girardi properly had him come out for the eighth inning, so that he could pitch to one batter and then leave the game, allowing for his own personal ovation from the Yankee Stadium crowd. That hitter stroked a double, however, only the second hit given up by the aging lefty, and Pettitte left to the cheers of an adoring crowd as reliever David Robertson made his way to the mound.

Perhaps this really was a scripted Hollywood movie. I have been talking for some time about how this is the end of an era, and that Rivera's retirement will signal a clear downturn in the fortunes of the Yankees. Robertson had, in the past, been anointed as the heir apparent to Rivera, the man who would take over as closer when the great Mariano finally called it quits. He has, thus far, failed miserably in his auditions for the job, however, and Sunday, if it were to be taken as such an audition, was no exception. Two batters later, the runner from second had crossed the plate and given the Giants a 2-1 lead. In a move which smacked of irony, Robertson was then lifted for Rivera, who again strode to the mound, this time to the recorded version of "*Enter Sandman*," and quickly recorded two outs to end the eighth inning.

The bottom of the eighth provided more Hollywood-style theatrics. The Yankees put runners on second and third with nobody out. In a "feel-good" movie, those two runners would cross the plate, giving the Yankees a lead which Rivera would protect in the top of the ninth, giving him a win on his special day. Alas, this was no such movie, but rather a harbinger of the nightmares that will no doubt plague the Yankee faithful for years to come. By the time that the dust had settled, the Yankees had not scored anything, and instead had two runners thrown out at the plate. Rivera then pitched a scoreless ninth but, alas, the home team was unable to muster any threat in the bottom of the ninth and the game ended with the final batter symbolically striking out, the Yankees on the short end of the 2-1 final score, with Andy Pettitte being charged with the loss despite surrendering only two hits in his 7+ innings of work. The loss left the Yankees four games out of the wild card race, with only six games left to play. This deficit seems insurmountable. There will be no post-season for New York in 2013.

Mariano Rivera throws what would be his last pitch of the game

On a grander scale, the retirement of both Rivera and Pettitte truly brings down the curtain on a miraculous era in Yankee, and baseball, history. Forget the five World Series rings that the "Core Four" captured, along with their more than a dozen consecutive post-season appearances. With the exception of Pettitte's three years in an Astros uniform, those two, along with Derek Jeter and recently-retired Jorge Posada, played together for almost two decades. In this era of escalating salaries, it is unlikely, no, it is impossible to imagine, that any group of teammates will stay together for such an extended period of time.

As for the Yankees, the reality that their fans must face is that they are now an average team, a group of aging, overpaid veterans coupled with a supporting cast of players on the downside of their careers and youngsters who likely should still be honing their skills in the minor leagues. The tremendous salaries being paid to such underperformers as Rodriguez, Sabathia, and Mark Teixeira have shackled the team's owners from amassing a better team, and their depleted farm system is incapable of providing the team with an influx of young talent. At least for the foreseeable future, it is clear that the Yankees will not be able to duplicate the successes of the Rivera-Jeter-Pettitte-Posada Yankees.

The weekend was, unquestionably, an emotional one. It was a bittersweet one. We celebrated the career of one of the game's all-time best performers, at the same time bidding farewell to both he and one of his long-time teammates. Some celebrated the accomplishments of the most reviled of Yankees, while others mourned his ascension to the top of a leader board once held by one of the most revered of all Yankees and ballplayers.

It also signaled, clearly, the end of an era.

Extra Innings: **Some say that I am prone to exaggeration. Perhaps that is true, but the retirements of Mariano Rivera and then Derek Jeter unquestionably brought down the curtain on a special era of baseball in the Bronx. The loss of those two men, the last remaining links to the glory days of the late 1990s and early 2000s, left a void not only for the Yankees but for baseball in general.**

September of 2015 brought a similar "end of an era" for Yankee fans with the news of the death of Yogi Berra. As I wrote on social media (I was no longer blogging at the time), his death meant that all of the true Yankee legends were now gone – leaving us with mere mortals. Think about it – take the following five players – Babe Ruth, Lou Gehrig, Joe DiMaggio, Mickey Mantle, and Yogi Berra. Now match them up against five players from any other team – no team can come close. In fact, take any group of five players (at the same positions) and the Yankee quintet will still likely be better. That is certainly not the case with the current crop of Yankees.

Is it Better to Have Played and Lost (In the Playoffs?)

(Originally posted October 4, 2013)

"Tis better to have loved and lost, then never to have loved at all ..." ---
Alfred, Lord Tennyson

Above are the words spoken thousands, if not millions of times, to people, especially heartbroken young women, after the breakup of their latest romance. It is a quote that everyone has either used or heard someone else use at least one time.

So I posit the following corollary question – *Is it better to have played and lost, then never to have played at all (in the playoffs, that is)?*

Monday, I had intended to post a blog about the baseball playoffs. In that post, I was going to compare and contrast two groups of players, like so:

Group A:

Bartolo Colon, SP, Oakland	*AJ Burnett, SP, Pitt*
Freddy Garcia, SP, Atlanta	*Kyle Farnsworth, RP, Pitt*
Phil Coke, RP, Det	*Russell Martin, C, Pitt*
Austin Jackson, OF, Det	*Nick Swisher, 1B, Cle*
Jason Giambi, DH, Cle	

BLOGGIN' BASEBALL II (FROM THE BLEACHERS) - ANDREW WOLFENSON

Group B:

CC Sabathia, SP, Yankees   Phil Hughes, SP, Yankees

Joba Chamberlain, RP, Yankees   Boone Logan, RP, Yankees

Curtis Granderson, OF, Yankees Mark Teixeira, 1B, Yankees

Alex Rodriguez, DH, Yankees

Then, I was going to "compare and contrast" them.

*****

Question 1 – *What do all of the above players have in common?* The answer is that they have all, at one time or another, played for the Yankees.

Question 2 – *What is the difference between the players in Group A and the players in Group B?* The answer, of course, is that all of the men in Group A are currently playing in the playoffs while the men in Group B, like the rest of the current Yankees, are home watching the games in their living rooms.

*****

I was then going to discuss how the Yankees' aging and too-often-injured roster cannot compete anymore, and that the large contracts given to several of the Group B players have prohibited the team's ownership from fielding a truly competitive team. Then, however, I would admit that, given the choice between the players in Group A and Group B, I would still likely choose Group B – because I shed no tears when the members of Group A were told that they could no longer wear the pinstripes, with the possible exception of Austin Jackson.

I was pleased when they refused to re-sign Nick Swisher and Russell Martin, both of whom, in my opinion, were seeking way too much money for their respective performances. I was ecstatic when they traded AJ Burnett. Jason Giambi was sent packing in the wake of a steroid scandal, so you can't possibly blame the team for cutting ties with him. So my conclusion would have been that the former Yanks were there in spite of themselves (in general), and due solely to the luck of being on particular teams.

Due to time constraints, I did not post, however, and, for one day, it looked like I had dodged a bullet. Former Yank Russell Martin crushed two home runs in the Wild Card game, leading the Pirates over the Reds and into a showdown with the Cardinals in the Division Series. In fairness to me, however, it should be pointed out that Martin had hit an identical number of round-trippers, two, in 33 previous post-season games. His power outburst, therefore, was quite unexpected. In fact, in three seasons with the Yankees, he played in fourteen post-season games, had only one home run, and managed only eight hits in 48 at bats, a measly .167 batting average.

The next day, the ex-Yankees totally reverted back to form. Nick Swisher went into Cleveland's playoff game against Tampa Bay with a career post-season average of about .190. Simple math tells us that all that he had to do in the game was get one hit in five at-bats to raise that average – and, not surprisingly, he failed to do so, going hitless in four at-bats to lower his career playoff/World Series average to a ghastly .165. A smug sense of satisfaction washes over me as I write this – *check my prior posts, where I begged the Yankees not to re-sign Swisher due to the fact that his bat disappears when the calendar page turns to October. This year, clearly, was no different.*

Then, last night, the Pirates sent AJ Burnett to the hill to face the Cardinals. If games only lasted two innings, then Burnett would have been golden. Alas, the teams are slated to play nine innings, and the third inning proved to be his undoing. In that fateful inning, the Cardinals scored a touchdown against Burnett – I mean; they scored *seven* runs off of him, putting the Pirates in a hole from which they could not recover. His pitching line was simply ugly – two innings, seven runs, six hits, four walks, and he even hit a guy. More smugness from this writer – *check my prior posts, where I begged the Yankees not to pitch Burnett in the post-season and then celebrated when he was shipped to Pittsburgh.*

So, I am left with my initial question - *Is it better to have played and lost, then never to have played at all (in the playoffs, that is)?*

Well, it is certainly better to not play as opposed to being completely embarrassed, as the Yankees were when they were swept and demoralized by Detroit in last year's post-season. On the other hand, teams like to trumpet their number of post-season appearances, and the players do make more money when their teams appear in the post-season.

Personally? It's probably better for my team not to play. Losing sucks. Losing when you are up all night watching the games, leaving you in a zombie-like catatonic state the next day, sucks even more. Last night, the Dodgers and Braves played in the late game – and at 11:00, they were only in the fifth inning. I had no qualms about turning the game off and going to sleep, because I have no "horse in the race," to use a cliché.

Thank you, Yankees, for not making the playoffs. My body thanks you. And tonight, may you feel able to go to sleep early as well, with no need to watch those silly teams in the playoffs – after all, only one can win the World Series. The rest will all be losers, and their fans will be left upset and extremely tired. Suckers.

Extra Innings: 2015 proved that it was better not to have played at all. The Yankees limped into the playoffs, qualifying for the Wild Card game against the Houston Astros. It is up for debate as to whether the Yankees actually played in the game, as they managed only three hits off of Houston ace Dallas Keuchel and came up on the short end of a 3-0 whitewash.

Why I Am Watching the Mets This Preseason...

(Originally posted March 6, 2014)

Baseball's spring training has begun in earnest and, thus far, this die-hard Yankees' fan has spent more time watching the Mets than his beloved Bronx Bombers. Why? Because hope springs eternal for every team come April and I am thinking of changing allegiances? No. Because so many of my friends root for the boys from Queens that I want to be a conformist and root for them also? No. Scouting for my fantasy baseball league? Uh, no.

The answer? Two words – Anthony Seratelli.

Anthony Seratelli may turn out to be one of major league baseball's "feel good" stories of 2014. The career minor-leaguer is attempting to reach the big leagues, as the Mets' backup shortstop, for the first time at the not-so-tender age of 31. This, in and of itself, would normally be enough for old guys like me to root for his success.

But wait, there's more.

Anthony Seratelli hails from Old Bridge, New Jersey, the suburban town where I grew up – my family moved there when I was little more than a year old, and we lived there for the next two decades. My hometown pride, therefore, overfloweth. And there's more – his aunt is one of the people with whom I grew up all those years ago.

My old hometown has not exactly made much good news in the past few years. To the contrary, any mention of Old Bridge in the newspapers has been negative – there was the horrible shooting at the Pathmark in 2012, the beating and murder in 2010 of Divyendu Singh by a pack of teenagers, and, infamously (and as I chronicled in a blog some time ago), resident Donna Simpson's attempt some

39

years ago to become the first woman to reach the not-so-svelte weight of one thousand pounds.

A positive story out of Old Bridge, therefore, would be much appreciated. Seratelli can be that story. The Mets are, according to published reports, actively considering him for the backup shortstop role, and, according to today's paper, his only hurdle now is to show the club that he can field the position properly (he played several positions last year in the Royals' system).

He's getting some good press (see articles from mlb.com and the *Star-Ledger*, below) and, with the beginning of the season a few short weeks away, his fate will be decided fairly soon. Here's hoping, on behalf of Old Bridge residents and old guys everywhere, that he makes it. And while the Mets may not be that good this year, another year of experience for their youngsters, especially the pitching staff, and the return of Matt Harvey following surgery in 2015 may make the team a pennant contender for years to come.

A 31-year old rookie? That's the stuff dreams are made of - and some dreams are just crazy enough to come true. Fingers crossed.

Extra Innings: Sadly, Seratelli did not make the Mets' final roster that season and did not step onto a major league diamond with any other team in this country. He did, however, go to Japan and play with the Seibu Lions during 2015.

The Yankees Celebrate Derek Jeter (Sadly, 2014 Style)

(Originally posted September 8, 2014)

Perhaps it was appropriate that the final score of yesterday's Yankees' game, on the day that they honored their Captain, Derek Jeter, was 2-0. Jeter wears uniform number 2, of course, and the day was meant to be a celebration and "thank you" for his twenty (2-0, get it?) years wearing pinstripes. And perhaps more appropriately, on this day where the Yankee family gathered to celebrate the career of their all-time greatest shortstop and a certain first-ballot Hall of Famer, the 2014 Yankees, a team which has struggled around the .500 mark all season, went down quietly to the suddenly relevant Kansas City Royals, a team much younger and better than the current incarnation of the Bronx Bombers.

Facing young flame-thrower Yordano Ventura (whose fastball often tops 100 mph) and three relievers, the once-mighty Yankees managed but four singles in the game, one by Jeter himself – the 3,450th hit of his illustrious career. That means that his teammates managed but three singles, combined, off of the quartet of Kansas City hurlers. Adding insult to injury, both Royals' runs in the game scored as a result of errors; thereby confirming the ineptitude with which the team performed on a day meant to honor their Captain.

The pundits had stressed that yesterday's ceremony was not a "goodbye" to Jeter, as there are three more weeks left in the regular season and then, for the completely delusional, the possibility of more games should the Yankees somehow make the playoffs. By having the ceremony yesterday, rather than September 21, the last Yankees' home game, the team ensured that the day would have more of a feeling of gratitude rather than of sorrowful farewells (and, of course, more ticket sales).

The last twelve months have been just that for the team, a year-long celebration of past successes wrapped around a season in which the team showed flashes of brilliance, but only to return down to their mediocre ways time and again. At the end of last season, the team gave its final salute to the greatest closer ever to ascend a baseball mound, Mariano Rivera, retiring his number 42 (he was the last player to ever wear the number which has already been retired by Major League Baseball in honor of Jackie Robinson) and having him take his proper place amongst the Yankee legends in the stadium's Monument Park. Then, this season, the team inexplicably hung plaques in that same Monument Park, a place once presumably reserved for greatness, to two cogs, not superstars, from its late 1990's dynasty – Tino Martinez and Paul O'Neill. Fans of the team can only wonder when the next round of plaques will be distributed – and other functional players from that era, like Charlie Hayes and Scott Brosius, are no doubt waiting by their phones with baited breath.

Yesterday's celebration was once again a reunion of the Yankee family, with O'Neill, Martinez, and other members of the recent World Series winning teams, such as Hideki Matsui and two fellow members of the "Core Four" – Rivera and Jorge Posada, on hand for the festivities. After introducing Jeter, the team then brought out three special guests – Cal Ripken, the man who revolutionized the shortstop position, Jeter's friend Michael Jordan, arguably the greatest basketball player ever and a fellow Nike spokesman, and former Yankee great and Hall of Famer Dave Winfield, who was introduced as being one of Jeter's idols and his inspiration for creating the "Turn 2 Foundation." No doubt Winfield trod onto the field wondering when his number 31 will be honored with a plaque in the newly-diminished Monument Park, at least alongside O'Neill's 21 and Martinez's 24 in the "also-rans" section.

The "thank you" to the Yankee Captain, however, also served as an unwitting homage, and "goodbye" to the Yankee team as some of us know it – the team that was once expected to compete for playoff spots and World Series berths every year, and a team which rarely disappointed. With Jeter's retirement, the entire "Core Four" is now gone – that foursome that proudly wore the Yankee uniform for the better part of two decades, a span unmatched in recent history. Rivera's number was retired last year, as noted above, and no doubt the next couple of years will bring us celebrations in honor of both Jorge Posada and Andy Pettitte, the other members of the group, as each gain their own plaques in the Monument Park. Maybe the plaques will be unveiled on the same day, so that the team is only forced to recognize its current mediocrity on only one occasion rather than two.

As currently constructed, the Yankees simple cannot compete. Aging, over-the-hill veterans have shackled the team with long-term, expensive contracts, and injuries to the elderly have forced the team, several times this season, to replace those players with career minor-leaguers. Unless the team is willing to blow open its vault as it has in years past and try to sign more All-Stars to join its aging corps next year, the team is destined to wallow in the middle of the standings for years to come – a team saddled not only with overpriced, aging veterans, but, perhaps more importantly, a barren minor-league system which seems incapable of churning out major league talent.

Meanwhile, teams built on youth, such as the Baltimore Orioles, Oakland A's, and the Royals, are ascending to the top of the American League standings. An old team like the Yankees simply cannot compete. They were unable to catch up with Ventura' fastballs yesterday and they will be unable to keep up with the young teams in years to come. So while the team billed yesterday's event as a "thank you" to its retiring Captain instead of a "goodbye," those of us who have followed and have rooted for the team over these past few decades know better – we know that yesterday's affair was grounded in gratitude not only to Jeter, but also to his former teammates, and it was truly a farewell to Yankee greatness, at least for now. It will be interesting to see what the future holds for the team, but anyone who expects great things from this team over the next few years is either not paying attention or is not grounded in reality.

I thank Derek Jeter for his tenure as Yankee shortstop and Captain. He brought a level of class to the game which is unmatched by but few of its current players, and leaves behind a legacy of winning which we will not likely see again in our lifetimes. He will be a certain first-ballot Hall of Famer at the turn of the decade, and stands as a beacon of light at a time when so many of his brethren were tainted by allegations of steroid use and of "me-first" attitudes. There are some players who play the game with Jeter-esque dignity and passion – Boston's Dustin Pedroia, the Twins' Joe Mauer, and the Mets' David Wright leap to mind – so here's hoping that others will follow - that they will play every day as if it is their last, will stay with teams for their entire careers so that the local fan base can better identify with them, and that they will let their on-the-field accomplishments define their legacy.

Extra Innings: Jeter's retirement left open the unofficial position of baseball ambassador, a role that nobody has yet stepped into. My belief was that the Mets' David Wright was the heir apparent to Jeter, a "good guy" who led one of the Big Apple's teams. Injuries have slowed Wright over the past couple of years and curtailed his statistics, but his reputation remains pristine and he finally ascended to the World Series in 2015. Even people who were not rooting for the Mets still found themselves rooting for Wright – any he was certainly deserving of such positive thoughts.

As for the post-Jeter Yankees, I think that this picture sums it up pretty well … a little post-apocalyptic feel to it, wouldn't you say?

BLOGGIN' BASEBALL II (FROM THE BLEACHERS) - ANDREW WOLFENSON

Jeter, A-Rod, and Ichiro - Hits, Respect, and Celebrations

(Originally posted September 28, 2014)

Today, Derek Jeter wrote the final chapter to the storybook ending that has been his last season with the Yankees – punctuating the saga with an infield single against the Red Sox, a hit which scored teammate Ichiro Suzuki from third base. Jeter and manager Joe Girardi then made the decision that it was time for Jeter to leave the game and exit the ball field, to the cheers of the Boston crowd and hugs from his teammates.

With that last single, Jeter finished his Hall of Fame career with 3,465 hits, placing him in sixth place on baseball's all-time hits list.

This total also places Jeter atop the leader board for "active" players (active as of this morning, that is), and the only current player to have reached the 3,000 hit plateau. Interestingly, the man who scored the run, Ichiro, has the third-most hits of any active player. As the curtain closed on the Yankees' 2014 season (and their latest era of success, but that's best saved for another day), Ichiro's MLB career hit total stood at 2,843 - although if one counts his 1,278 hits while playing in Japan, he is well over 4,000 career hits. A couple of years ago, 3,000 major league hits seemed a reasonable goal for the Japanese superstar. Relegated to a part-time role with the Yankees, however, the chances of his joining the iconic "3,000 hit club" while wearing Yankee pinstripes seem to have faded to zero.

Before Jeter stroked his 3,000[th] hit in 2011, no Yankee had ever joined the group's ranks – players like Wade Boggs, Rickey Henderson, and Dave Winfield spent time with the team, but had clubbed (Boggs' number 3,000, like Jeter's was a home run) or stroked their historic hit while wearing another team's uniforms. And when Jeter attained his entry hit, it seemed possible that the next two players

47

who could join the ranks might also do so while wearing Yankee pinstripes. Ichiro was one of those two, and the other was …

Alex Rodriguez.

As it stands now, baseball's active hits leaders, including Jeter, are as follows:

Derek Jeter	**3,465**
Alex Rodriguez	**2,939**
Ichiro Suzuki	**2,843**

Reports are that Rodriguez, who was suspended for the entire 2014 season, recently passed his physical and is ready to return to the field for 2015. A year ago, it seemed unfathomable that the Yankees would welcome their anti-hero back to the Bronx, but it now appears that the team, which is starved for a storyline after riding the retirement stories of Mariano Rivera and Jeter over the past two seasons, will be doing just that. A veritable parade of third basemen have attempted to fill Rodriguez' steroid-enlarged shoes over the past two seasons, with little to no success. The latest person to occupy the "hot corner," Chase Headley, is a free agent at the end of this season – when one considers the hitting numbers that he posted following his arrival in New York this season, and the fact that Rodriguez is still under contract, it does not seem to make sense for the team to throw millions of dollars at Headley – especially when the team's brass is already charged with replacing its shortstop – the position that Jeter manned for the past 20 years.

Plus, Rodriguez stands a paltry 61 hits away from 3,000. Assuming that Ichiro continues to play part-time, it will take at least three years for him to reach the magic number, assuming he continues to play that long. The next player with a legitimate chance at reaching this career milestone appears to be Albert Pujols of the Angels, who stands almost 500 hits shy and is also at least three or four years away from reaching such baseball immortality. For the Yankees, a team facing another playoff-less season, the loss of the last member of its "core four," and boasting a line-up devoid of any other iconic players, welcoming A-Rod back into the fold and watching him join the ranks of the 3,000 hit club could be just the public relations boon that the team requires – even if the publicity is anti-Rodriguez. People will still flock to the stadium to watch the chase, even if they are booing him. Either way, it translates to dollars for the team.

Rodriguez had a front seat for the Mariano Rivera Farewell Tour of 2013. He was there for the day held in Rivera's honor, and witnessed, first-hand, the love that a team and fans could show for one of its favorite players. As he was exiled this season, he was not present for Jeter's farewell tour, and was not in the various stadiums as teams honored Jeter and showered him with gifts. He was not in the Stadium for Derek Jeter Day earlier this month, and was not in the Stadium last Thursday night to witness Jeter's remarkable, Hollywood-scripted walk-off single to beat the Orioles in his last Yankee Stadium at-bat. He was not in Fenway Park, enemy territory, today to witness Jeter, in his final major league at-bat, single to drive in Ichiro with the Yankees' third run in what would eventually be a season-ending 9-5 victory.

No doubt, however, Rodriguez heard the cheers – if fact, even if he was not watching the games, no doubt he somehow "felt" the cheers and the roar of the crowds. He heard the adulation showered upon Jeter from coast to coast, saw the checks given to Jeter's "Turn 2 Foundation", and the "RE2PECT" video prepared by Nike. He heard the laudatory comments from players, fans, and celebrities for Jeter, and watched his former best friend and current rival bask in the glow of glory and respect that has been reserved for so few players before him, at levels unmatched in this generation. And it was all earned by Jeter, widely regarded as the classiest ballplayer of his time, and well-deserved.

And no doubt Rodriguez sat at home, wondering to himself how much of the love and adulation given to both Rivera and Jeter would be passed on to him. He likely wondered if, when he took his last at-bats in a major league ballpark, whether he would do so as a member of the Yankees and, if he did so, would the Yankee family return to the Stadium to fete him, as they had for Jeter? Would former players like Rivera, Jorge Posada, Andy Pettitte, and Tino Martinez come back for him, as they did last week for Jeter? Would his old manager, Joe Torre, return to the Bronx, as he did for Jeter? Would the hated Red Sox, led by their own iconic player, David Ortiz, hold a ceremony for him as they did for Jeter this afternoon? And would the Boston faithful cheer for him and chant his name in a friendly manner, as they did this past weekend for Jeter?

Likely not. This, despite the fact that the *Newark Star-Ledger*, in today's edition, ranked the Top 25 Yankees of All-Time; Jeter finished at number six *(numbers buffs should note that Jeter was picked sixth overall in the 1992 amateur draft by the Yankees, and, as noted above, he finished his career at number six on the all-time hits list)*. Rodriguez, meanwhile, came in at number 13, coincidentally his uniform number. All twelve of the players listed above him, as well as six of those rounding out the Top 25, have plaques in Yankee Stadium's Monument Park. Four of the players listed below him have had their uniform numbers retired by the Yankees.

Yet, it is far-fetched to think that the Yankees will conduct an "Alex Rodriguez Day" irrespective of whether he reaches 3,000 hits while in pinstripes, and regardless of whether he slugs the 46 more home runs he needs to reach another iconic level, that of 700 home runs (with seven more home runs, he passes Willie Mays on the all-time list and will be in fourth place all-time, behind only fellow steroid-user Barry Bonds, Hank Aaron, and Babe Ruth). Equally unlikely would be placement of a plaque in hallowed Monument Park, as well as retirement of A-Rod's number 13.

So, in essence, the Yankees will be using Alex Rodriguez, should he begin the 2015 season as the team's third baseman. They will be using him for the purposes of increasing ticket sales and the resulting rise in concession and memorabilia revenues, riding his coattails as he continues his assaults on baseball's hallowed numbers. They will use him in much the same way that he has used PED's to increase his personal revenues – because A-Rod, as it is widely stated, is all about the numbers – his numbers. It is all about his statistics and his place among baseball's elite.

In sharp contrast stands Derek Jeter. Over a 20-year career, he amassed the sixth-most hits of any player to step onto a major league ball field. He was a five-time World Series winner. He holds numerous Yankee hitting records, and was recently ranked by ESPN as the third-best shortstop of all time. Derek Jeter, however, was the consummate team player – he wanted to win, and did what he did on the field not for personal accolades, but to further the team's interests. What makes Derek Jeter a sure-fire first-ballot Hall of Famer, it has been said time and again, is not these statistics – what makes Jeter special, and has unquestionably stamped his ticket for the Hall, is his leadership, the way that he played the game by example and how he made those around him better. The other night, former opponent Curt Schilling noted that not one person in baseball has a bad thing to say about Derek Jeter. Not a teammate, an opponent, a manager, owner – anyone.

That is why he has been celebrated for so long, and why he was lauded in every city in which the Yankees played this season, his farewell season. It is a lesson that Rodriguez never seemed to understand. And it is the reason that you will not see a farewell tour for Rodriguez, even if he never fully comprehends why.

It is a matter of respect. Whether you spell the word with an "s" or a "2", Derek Jeter has earned such respect/r2spect from teammates, opponents, and fans alike. No other player of this generation has earned such respect, and Alex

Rodriguez's actions, often, have had quite the opposite effect on how others view him.

Extra Innings: **Rodriguez joined the 3,000 hit fraternity in grand style, joining Jeter and Wade Boggs as the only major leaguers to slug a home run for their milestone hit. While Rodriguez and his teammates celebrated on the field, however, it was months before the team officially honored the accomplishment. As for Ichiro, he went to South Florida to play for the Marlins and enters the 2016 season with 2,935 hits – making him a lock to reach the milestone in 2016. That is, of course, in addition to the 1,278 hits that he tallied while playing in the Japanese League.**

CHAPTER 2 – ALEX RODRIGUEZ

OJ Simpson. Casey Anthony. George Zimmerman. Alex Rodriguez

(Originally posted July 31, 2013)

OJ Simpson. Casey Anthony. George Zimmerman. Alex Rodriguez.

All four have been tried and convicted in the court of public opinion. Three have been acquitted, by a jury, of the crimes that of which they were accused. The fourth may hear his judgment announced tomorrow, but there will be no exoneration from a jury for his alleged transgressions.

Granted, the infractions that Rodriguez is alleged to have committed pale in comparison with those of the other three:

-- One, an African-American celebrity ex-athlete, *allegedly* murdered his white ex-wife and another individual, whom he *allegedly* believed was her lover; One *allegedly* murdered her daughter; One, a white-Hispanic vigilante, *allegedly* murdered an African-American teenager --

Realistically, *allegedly* taking some steroids or other Performance-enhancing drugs cannot be compared to murder. This is especially true when race relations are involved, as in two of the scenarios above, or where the *alleged* murderer is the victim's own mother. The salacious *allegations* and media coverage of all of these cases led to public outcries of guilt for each, but such outcries did not carry over into the courtrooms for any of them.

OJ Simpson was eventually acquitted by a jury in California. But he did kill Nicole Brown Simpson and Ron Goldman, right? Ask anyone – well, more to the point – ask any white person. There was (and likely still is) a large group of

African-Americans who protested that OJ *was innocent*, and that he was falsely accused based on his race. As one woman stated while being interviewed for a TV news segment after the verdict was announced, and clearly referring to the Juice's prior appearance in ads for Hertz rent-a-car, "*I always knew that that nice man running through the airport couldn't have done it.*"

Casey Anthony was eventually acquitted by a jury in Florida. But she did kill her daughter, right? Ask anyone.

George Zimmerman was eventually acquitted by a jury in Florida. But he did murder Trayvon Martin, right? Ask, well, many people.

These three people stand as the starkest examples of persons convicted by public opinion, although all were acquitted following a jury trial in which, presumably, the evidence was presented in an even-handed manner, untouched by media bias. Two of these people are currently walking the streets; Simpson, of course, was later convicted by a Las Vegas jury of false imprisonment in what can best be termed as a "we finally got you" verdict of retribution, not unlike when Al Capone went to jail for tax evasion.

So now we are left with Alex. The media would have us believe that Alex Rodriguez was one of the biggest clients of the latest steroid-factory, Biogenesis, a man who not only used Performance-Enhancing drugs, but also is *alleged* to have facilitated other players in obtaining such substances, a man who *allegedly* sought to hinder Major League Baseball's investigation into drug use by its players, a man who *allegedly* tried to purchase documents which would have incriminated him and/or a man who *allegedly* sought to buy the testimony of others in order to protect his name. The media is opining (perhaps based on credible information, but who knows?) that baseball has offered Alex a suspension deal whereby he would be suspended for the remainder of the 2013 season, as well as the entire 2014 season. If he does not accept that suspension, it is said, then the lords of baseball will seek a lifetime ban against the former MVP, based not only on his

56

alleged violation of baseball's anti-drug policy, but also, in an unprecedented use of the commissioner's powers, on his *alleged* violations of baseball's collective bargaining agreement.

The lords of baseball, we are led to believe, have such a mountain of evidence against A-Rod that they believe that such a suspension/ban would pass judicial muster should it be appealed.

The lords of baseball, clearly, want Alex Rodriguez out of their sport. His employer, the Yankees, clearly want Alex Rodriguez out of the sport. Other players, suddenly imbued with a "holier than thou" attitude and what appears to be a new-found desire to rid the sport of drug users, clearly want Alex Rodriguez out of the sport. Members of the media, despite their recent calls for Alex to return and at least play a decent third place for the sputtering Yankees, clearly want Alex Rodriguez out of the sport. The Yankee faithful, who have suffered through his shenanigans since his arrival in the Bronx, clearly want Alex Rodriguez out of the sport.

All of which leads to the inevitable public conviction of Alex Rodriguez – although, we should note, all of the cries for suspension are based on *allegations.* Yes, he admitted to using illegal substances back in 2001-2003 when he was playing for Texas, an admission for which he received no suspension or other penalty from the league – but the public has not been supplied with even one document, one shred of evidence, to support MLB's contentions that Alex Rodriguez *allegedly* violated any of baseball's rules or laws since that time. That Ryan Braun voluntarily accepted a suspension can be used as more *circumstantial evidence* against Rodriguez, but just because Braun clearly admits using improper substances, even though it strengthens the credibility of Biogenesis' owner, Tony Bosch, and his record-keeping, does not mean that Rodriguez was also involved.

Having said that, one would think that we should, perhaps, pity poor Alex Rodriguez rather than vilify him.

But that would run counter to the real reason that the Yankees, and the team's fans, should clearly want Alex Rodriguez out of the sport - but for a different reason. Wait, let's change that last sentence to reflect the reality of the situation – "But that would run counter to the real reason that the Yankees, and the team's fans, should clearly want Alex Rodriguez out of pinstripes!"

The Yankees management, Yankee players, and fans are not suddenly embarking on a new "anti-drug" campaign – to the contrary, to anyone associated with or who root for the Bronx Bombers, this is a much simpler matter – a decision borne not of a desire to rid the team of a drug user, but rather to rid the team of a $30 million a year albatross. It has been reported that more suspensions will be announced this week, perhaps as early as tomorrow. And if Nelson Cruz is suspended, Texas Rangers' management and fans will be upset. If Jhonny Peralta is suspended, Tigers' brass and fans will be upset; in fact, the team traded for a shortstop yesterday as a precautionary measure. If any other member of the alleged Biogenesis client list is suspended, their team and fan base will be irate.

So why is it different for Rodriguez? The fact that he has been disliked by players, both on his own team and opponents, plays a factor. Also, the fact that he has been tabloid fodder and has never truly been accepted by a Yankee fan base that already has a player to adore, Derek Jeter, does as well. The constant on-again-off-again accusations of steroid use have made an already tenuous relationship between Rodriguez and the fans even worse, and his proclamations of being ready to play, even when he had not been examined by team doctors (or, as we later discovered, even his own doctor) have further strained his relationship with Yankee brass. But if he were slated to make only $7 million dollars in 2014, and could still hit 25 home runs and knock in 90 runs per season, he would be welcomed back with open arms.

Apparently Alex now wants to be a "role model" as reported in this week's issue of *Sports Illustrated*. Can you hear the collective snickering across the New York area?

The problem is that he is due salaries well in excess of the above figure – a whopping $30 million or so per year. 2014 is an important "salary cap" year – any team that has salaries in excess of $189 million for the 2014 season is subject to being hit with large monetary penalties. The Yankees have pledged to stay at or below that amount, hence the parade of minor-leaguers who have shuttled between the farm system and the Bronx this year to replace the Yankees' gaggle of injured starters. But keeping the payroll below $189 million, especially when a team has about $100 million of that tied up in four players already (Rodriguez, Jeter, CC Sabathia and Mark Teixeira) is extremely difficult – so if the $30 million man was removed from the roster, and his salary removed from the payroll, the team could go out and sign a couple of quality players. Hence, the desires of the team and its fan base to have a suspension levied.

The desires, however, are based on mere *allegations*. We do not know, as fans, what A-Rod *allegedly* did, other than a general statement that he *allegedly* purchased PED's from Biogenesis. And mere *allegations* cannot be enough to sustain baseball's *allegedly* intended courses of action – nor can mere *allegations* be sufficient for the world to convict Alex Rodriguez of violating baseball's drug policy and/or Collective Bargaining Agreement, right?

Perhaps. Then again, sometimes the public does get it right. As a Yankees' fan, of course, I hope that this is one of those times. Tomorrow may be the day that the shackles can come off of the Yankee ownership's suddenly tight wallets. Neither Casey Anthony nor George Zimmerman is currently "locked up" despite the overwhelming belief of many in their guilt. The Yankees and their fans do not need to be locked up in mediocrity due to the actions of their $30 million superstar, a man who continued to use steroids even after his *mea culpa* apology some years ago. *Allegedly.*

Extra Innings: George Zimmerman was unable to stay out of trouble, and did eventually get locked up. That meant that two of the people from this blog

served time or are serving time – OJ and Zimmerman. Casey Anthony is still walking the streets, although we're not quite sure which streets. And Alex? Read on.

A-Rod's Return to the Yankees - The Saga Continues

(Originally posted August 5, 2013)

The hammer fell today, as expected. Major League Baseball has suspended a dozen players as punishment for their participation in the Biogenesis scandal, and they join former MVP Ryan Braun in the latest cadre of baseball's rogues, those who will serve for all-time as the faces of the ills that continued to plague baseball even after the "steroid era" had allegedly been brought to a conclusion. Most of those punished have, as expected, taken their lumps and will now sit out the rest of the season, a convenient way that the Lords of Baseball have utilized the 50-game ban available to them under baseball's anti-drug policy.

One player, also not unexpectedly, has seen fit to challenge the powers that be, a solitary renegade hell-bent on pursuing his mission to prove that he is capable of being the most important, or at least the most polarizing, figure that the game has seen in years.

That lone holdout, of course, is Alex Rodriguez. He was hit with the biggest suspension, totaling about 210 games (the remainder of this season, effective Thursday, and all of next season) and has vowed that he will not only fight the suspension, but that he will prevail.

One can only think that the Lords of Baseball have some level of confidence in their actions, that Commissioner Bud Selig and his cabinet members truly believe that they have sufficient evidence to banish A-Rod from the game for such an extended period of time. While the suspension is based solely on the drug policy and not on the possibly overreaching "best interests of the game," the fact that Alex's suspension was significantly longer than the others must mean that the allegations are also much stronger – remember, he has never before been suspended under the drug policy - so technically, this should be his first offense (despite his prior admission) and therefore warrant a 50-game suspension only – unless there is something more that they can prove against him.

So, faced with the presumed mountain of evidence, why wouldn't A-Rod simply negotiate a resolution (like Braun before him) and quietly accept his fate? Why wouldn't he simply accept the suspension, and not force baseball into what promises to be a messy separation, if not divorce? Why not quietly go away and then return, perhaps triumphantly, in 2015, proving that he is capable of playing at a high level even without the use of performance-enhancing drugs?

There are no simple answers. First, start with the proposition that Alex Rodriguez does nothing quietly. This was quite in evidence lately as he essentially sparred with the team and its ownership, allegedly hiring his own doctor to show that he was capable of playing and then accusing the Yankees and MLB of conspiring to remove him from pinstripes. This is the man who went through a messy divorce after dalliances with a variety of women in other cities was revealed, dated Madonna, has admitted to prior use of Performance-Enhancing drugs, has signed not one, but two, mind-boggling contracts, who has also dated actresses Kate Hudson and Cameron Diaz (popcorn, anyone?) and who was once poised to shatter all of baseball's slugging records until injuries, and investigations, intervened.

Two overwhelming "truths" to consider – first, that he obtained and used PED's from Biogenesis, and second, that few people, if any, want him to return to the playing field. The first seems fairly certain – the silence of the others in accepting their suspensions, and the silence of the Players' Association in not challenging or disputing any of the allegations speaks volumes as to the credibility of the charges. So even though he should be considered innocent until proven guilty, it is pretty safe to say that the reverse is true. As for the second, despite the calls of some that a healthy A-Rod is a better option than the sequence of pretenders that the Yankees have sent out to third base this year, the team does not want him back - too much distraction, too little production, and, most critically, too much money being spent for a man who will likely be, at best, an average player.

No doubt Alex's excuse for what he has done, and the substances that he has put into his body, is that he was doing what he thought to be best to help the team. We would have to take that with a grain of salt, as many would argue that Alex is always about Alex and his own statistics. But even if we assume his reason to be true, then isn't he doing just the opposite here? The media circus that will now consume the Yankees, far worse than any circus surrounding Rodriguez in the past, will toll the death knell for the Yankees' chances at the post-season this year – slim though they may now be. And then, assuming he continues to play until the appeal is heard (possibly September), then, afterward, if the suspension is upheld, he will be out for 2014 and half of 2015 (unless the length of the suspension is decreased or increased) - then what will have been accomplished? He will have put some millions more dollars into his pocket, but does he really need the money?

He will be heckled wherever he goes – even in the Bronx – so the desire for adulation cannot be the reasons for his petulance. And 50 games, assuming he makes it to the end of this season, will not be sufficient to pad his statistics enough to reach his eventual goals – he is still about 100 hits shy of the magic 3,000 figure, and will not reach that level this year. He sits in fifth place on the all-time homers list, and does not pose a serious threat his predecessor PED user and denier, Barry Bonds.

Nothing with Alex Rodriguez has been easy, at least since his joining the Yankees almost a decade ago. That does not appear to be likely to change now. If and when his eventual guilt is revealed, the resulting expulsion may prove to bar him from the game forever; and the doors of the Hall of Fame will similarly slam in his face so at what cost is this latest act in the saga that is A-Rod?

The real question is - which other disgraced player will A-Rod eventually most resemble?

Will he be Ryan Braun? Will he deny, deny, deny until one day he simply accepts his fate, tacitly confirming that the suspicions and allegations lodged against him were true?

Will he be Barry Bonds, continuing to deny knowledge of his transgressions and seeking to blame any ingestion of improper materials on others, much like he did with his prior admission of using improper substances between 2001 and 2003?

Or will he be Roger Clemens, overconfident and defiant to the end, yet still considered guilty by all associated with the game?

It really does not matter. All of those three are considered cheaters. As of now, none seems capable of rehabilitating the tarnished reputations caused by the alleged PED use, and the Hall of Fame, as yet, has not seen fit to admit anyone even linked to the use of steroids or PED's. So in the end, his fate will be the same as those three – a player who amassed tremendous statistics and won awards, but who did so with the use of synthetic and improper substances. He will eventually retire or be forced from baseball, leaving behind the question of how much he could have done had he stayed clean – and that, sadly, will be the only real debate about his career and his legacy.

His first at-bat is done. He was booed loudly by the Chicago crowd, and responded by blooping a single to left field. It was a far cry from the homer that he blasted in his first at-bat (in Baltimore) upon returning from injury several years ago, and may serve as a harbinger for the new, not-so-powerful, natural Alex Rodriguez.

Three days ago, the Yankee family recalled one of its greatest tragedies, the death of Captain and leader Thurman Munson in 1979. Today, the latest chapter, but by no means the last chapter, or a different Yankee tragedy is being played out. This tragedy, like the Greek tragedies written so long ago, id playing out on a grand stage over a period of time. And like so many protagonists in those

Greek tragedies, it will be Alex Rodriguez's hubris which will prove to be his ultimate undoing.

Extra Innings: Rodriguez's return to the diamond was far better than anyone could have anticipated. He essentially carried the team on his back for the first half of the season, and finished 2015 with 33 home runs and 86 RBI. Many viewed him as a legitimate candidate for "Comeback Player of the Year" honors, and some believe that he did not win the award due to the circumstances which led up to the need for him to "come back".

My Dinner with Bud Selig and Alex Rodriguez

(Originally posted August 15, 2013)

Last night, I had the pleasure of sitting down for dinner with the two people who are the center of the latest steroid controversy to rock major league baseball, MLB Commissioner Bud Selig and accused PED user Alex Rodriguez. With their permission, I taped the conversation and a partial transcript of same follows below.

Andy (AW):   Thank you both for joining me. I know that you both have very hectic schedules and this is a very touchy subject for each of you.

Bud (BS):   It is my pleasure, Andy. I have read your previous blogs with great interest and you seem to have the right ideas about certain things (winks at me) so this seemed an appropriate time to talk.

Alex (AR):   Yes, thank you for having me. I see that you have said nothing but nice things about me in the past, like all of those fans who were cheering for me when I returned to Yankee Stadium, so I really couldn't wait to meet you and thank you for your support.

BS: Really, Alex? Have you read Andy's posts in the past? I don't think that they have been complimentary at all – he calls you all sorts of names and has said that the team should get rid of you.

AR: I don't know what posts you were reading, Bud. I see nothing but positives in there.

AW: (Glaring at Bud) It doesn't really matter what he has read, OK? The important thing is that we are all here together now, so let's talk about what's going on. Mr. Selig, why don't you start?

BS: OK, Andy, I will. I don't want to make this sound too rehearsed, but the simple fact is that we, meaning all of major league baseball, are intent on ridding the sport of cheaters and those who use performance-enhancing drugs. All of the players want the cheaters out, the owners want the cheaters out, and the league office, of course, wants to protect the integrity of the game.

AW: I am intrigued by that last statement, Bud. Can I call you Bud? (he nods approvingly). You speak of the integrity of the game; but didn't the owners and players essentially turn a blind eye to the steroid use when it benefitted the game? When Mark McGwire and Sammy Sosa, looking like white and tan versions of the Incredible Hulk, were blasting homer after homer into the seats, what was baseball doing then?

AR: You mean other than collecting money? Look, Andy, here's my problem. If Barry Bonds had not done steroids, I would be seven homers closer to the all-time record. Look it up. Hank Aaron hit 755. Bonds has 762. That means I will need seven more homers to break the record, which I would not have needed if Bonds had not done steroids.

Both Selig and I look at Rodriguez, incredulous. A dramatic pause follows.

AR: You know what I mean, right? The same is true for RBI. I am in sixth place now, but would be in fifth if not for Bonds, that cheater. It's just not fair, you know.

Selig and I look at Rodriguez, who seems deadly serious. We then look at each other, and Selig shrugs his shoulders.

BS: You see what I have to deal with?

AW: We will get to that in a second, Bud. You still haven't answered my question.

BS: Andy, you have to understand. Baseball was in grave danger prior to Mark and Sammy's chase for Roger Maris' single-season home run record. We had just come off of the strike, fans weren't coming to the ballpark, and we needed some excitement. And that Sammy Sosa was just so lovable. Always smiling, talking in his funny accent. How could you not love him? It's like David Ortiz now – I'm not saying that he is using or has used steroids, but look at him. Just look at him. He's like a hulking teddy bear, always in a good mood and smiling. The game needs more players like that.

AW: So are you admitting that the ownership and league knew about the PED use back then and simply chose to do nothing about it because it benefitted the game?

BS: Don't be silly. I would never admit to that.

AW: But you just said …

BS: Listen, it does not matter now. All that we are talking about now is getting rid of the abusers today. We took great strides toward doing so with our latest suspensions, and everyone took their poison like a man, except for Alex here. We wanted it all to go away. I don't know why he just won't play along.

AW: Tell me, how did you get everyone else to agree? It is a little surprising that you would get over a dozen players to suspensions, don't you think? And not have the Players' Association complain?

BS: Well, Andy, I will tell you – first, we went to Braun. I sat down with Ryan at a deli – remember, I used to own the Brewers and we are both Jews, so I like to think that we have a nice relationship. I said to him, "Ryan, be a *mensch*. I need you to take one for the league's benefit. I am getting all sorts of *tsoris* from everyone, it's making me *meshugganah*." And he thought about it and agreed to be the first one – of course, the fact that he is hurt and the Brewers really suck this year didn't hurt any. And most of the guys were either hurt or in the minors, so they were easy. And the Latin Americans, we just told them that we would have their visas revoked so they would be deported (chuckles lightly).

AR: What does *tsoris* mean?

AW: It means misery, annoyance.

BS: Kind of like what you're giving us right now.

AR: I don't know what you are talking about.

At that point, Alex reached for his right ear and cupped it with his hand, leaning forward and murmuring "what? I can't hear you." He removed his hand, and I could see a small earpiece embedded into his ear.

AW: Alex, are you wearing an earpiece? Who is talking to you?

AR: This earpiece? Oh, it's my attorneys. I am paying them so much money it's ridiculous, so I don't even take a crap without them telling me anymore.

AW: So they can hear everything we say and they are telling you what to say?

AR: I guess so. Certainly you don't think anything that I have said since I lied about getting the second medical opinion has been on my own.

AW: Well, that kind of defeats the purpose of this conversation, but let's try anyway. Why are you appealing the suspension?

AR: (lifting his head as if listening to someone and then speaking deliberately) Andy, I am appealing the suspension because I am innocent. I have not used PED's. I did not try to buy documents or witnesses. Baseball is being very unfair to me. I want to be a role model to my children, and to accept a suspension for something that I did not do would be wrong.

AW: Well spoken, Alex. Do you really believe that?

AR: Believe what?

AW: What you just said.

AR: What did I say again?

I looked over at Selig and smiled before continuing.

AW: You said that you are appealing the suspension because you don't want to lose the money.

AR: Yes, that's right.

Rodriguez jolted backward, as if someone was yelling in his ear. He again placed his hand over his ear, bent forward, and said, audibly, "I don't care what you say. I'm the client. I will say what I want." He ripped the earpiece out of his ear and threw it to the ground.

AR: Of course it is about the money. And the records. I am going to be the all-time Home Run king, you know. I'm going to pass Willie soon, and next year, I'm going to pass Babe Ruth and then it's on to Aaron and Bonds.

AW: You sure seem to know your stats.

AR: Of course I do, Andy. It's all about me and my numbers. You should know that by now. I don't give a damn about the game or the Yankees. It's all about Alex. It's always been all about me. (He stares directly at Bud Selig and lowers his voice) I am bigger than the game, Bud. Don't you ever forget it.

BS: How are you bigger than the game?

AR: You're kidding me, right? People come to see me. They want to see me break records. They cheer me wherever I go. Look in the newspapers – article after article about me. Article after article saying, "come back Alex, we want you back." I'm the biggest thing in baseball since Babe Ruth. Baseball can't survive without Alex Rodriguez.

BS: You're wrong, Alex. It's not all about you. It's about the integrity of the game, which you are ruining by this appeal.

AR: Just wait, then. I'm going to sue baseball, you know. I have my high-powered litigators now, and they are going to sue you for persecuting me.

At that moment, three men in suits burst into the restaurant, calling for Rodriguez. He excused himself, walked over to them, and had an animated conversation with them before waving them out of the establishment. "I pay your bills," he called after them, "you listen to me. I am Alex Rodriguez. I am bigger than all of you."

AR: (settling back in his chair) Sorry about that. Lawyers, can't stand them. They're as bad as used car salesman.

AW: Alex, you know that Bud was a car dealer and that's how he made the money to buy the Brewers, right?

AR: Really? I did not know that. Well, no offense, Bud.

BS: None taken. What offends me is that you are trying to ruin the game.

AR: You are trying to ruin me. Think about it, how great would it be if I hit the record-breaking home run in Yankee Stadium, baseball's biggest stage? Think of the ratings, think of the merchandising.

BS: Hmmm. Ratings? Merchandising money? I don't know if we have thought this through. Excuse me for a minute, fellas.

Selig stood and walked off to the side, his cell phone to his ear.

AW: That was interesting. Do you really think you can break the records?

AR: Of course I can, Andy, as long as they keep letting me use the juice. I can't do it on my own. I mean, I am the best, but even the best need a little help sometimes.

Selig returns to the table and sits down.

BS: Tell you what, Alex. How about we forget about this suspension thing? You don't bring any lawsuit, and I will talk to (Yankee owner Hal) Steinbrenner and (Yankee GM Brian) Cashman about having you back without any restrictions. And no more of those silly drug tests. You just keep hitting those homers. We don't want cheats like Bonds having records, right (smiling)?

AR: That's all I have ever wanted, Mr. Selig.

Selig and Rodriguez both grin and vigorously shake hands. Selig grimaces as he withdraws his hand.

BS: That's a really firm handshake, Alex. I think you may have broken my hand.

AR: Don't worry. I've got someone who can take care of the pain for you. I will give you his number.

Extra Innings: Sadly, this was a fictional conversation. Rodriguez's suspension, however, was not fiction and he sat out the entire 2014 season. He returned with a vengeance in 2015, defying all of his naysayers en route to a 33 home run, 86 RBI season. The bulk of these statistics were accumulated in the first half of the season, and Rodriguez's age did catch up to him over the final couple of months. He finished the season with a feeble outing in the 2015 Wild Card game, going 0-4 with two strikeouts.

Alex Rodriguez - Anti-Semite??

(Originally posted August 13, 2013)

Is Alex Rodriguez anti-Semitic? The Yankee slugger has been called many things over the past decade in New York, but, to my knowledge, he has never been fingered as a hater of the Jews. In light of recent events surrounding baseball and its investigation into PED use and the Biogenesis clinic, however, it is possible that this may be the next bombshell.

It's a simple application of what is known in math as the transitive property. You know, the one that provides that if A = B, and if B = C, then A must equal C. Confused? Don't be. Here's the scenario:

A.   Rumor has it that Rodriguez was the person who (this time) ratted out Brewers' slugger and former MVP Ryan Braun to major league baseball. According to sources, the original Biogenesis documents received by MLB were redacted and did not include Braun's name. Later, Rodriguez (or his representatives) obtained copies of ledgers with Braun's name and turned them over to MLB.

B.   According to baseball insider Buster Olney, Braun contacted several players during his prior (2012) investigation into possible steroid use and sought their support. As part of his pitch to the players, Braun allegedly told them that the tester who reported his positive drug test was anti-Semitic, and his hatred of Jews was the reason for his allegations of drug use by Braun.

So, to recap -

A.   Rodriguez ratted out Braun, and

B.   The prior person who notified MLB of Braun's drug use was labeled by Braun as an anti-Semite.

Therefore:

C.   It is only a matter of time before Braun alleges that Rodriguez, in addition to being a habitual PED user, is also anti-Semitic.

Rodriguez stated that the continuing saga surrounding his suspension will have bigger news in the future, didn't he? Maybe this is what he meant. Stay tuned. Remember, you read it here first.

Legal disclaimer - of course, I do not think that Alex Rodriguez is anti-Semitic and am not alleging with any seriousness that he is, nor do I think that Ryan Braun will level such allegations. I certainly do not want to trivialize the issue of anti-Semitism, which I have written about in the past and which is currently a hot-button topic on this very site. This post is merely meant to underscore the ridiculousness of the situations regarding both Braun and Rodriguez, situations which continue to do little more than embarrass both the players and major league baseball as a whole.

Extra Innings: I was kidding. Really.

Alex Rodriguez Plays the Media for Fools

(Originally posted August 22, 2013)

The media is reporting that Alex Rodriguez has instructed his legal team to stop the rhetoric about his case so that he can focus on playing baseball. The media is reporting this in a matter-of-fact tone, accepting, perhaps tacitly applauding him, for his actions.

As Bugs Bunny would say, what a bunch of maroons.

Start with three fundamental premises:

1.   Alex Rodriguez never has and never will say anything that was not, is not, or will not be completely self-serving.

2.   Alex Rodriguez's legal team is extremely well-paid, and they are calling all of the shots with respect to dissemination of information and misinformation – and they will not listen to him if he tells them to stop the media assault.

3.   This is the most important – Alex Rodriguez has absolutely nothing to gain from continuing to wage a war in the press against the Yankees or Major League Baseball.

Think about it. Since the time that A-Rod's suspension was first announced, either he and/or his legal team have put forth the following propositions:

1.   Major League Baseball and Commissioner Bud Selig have completely overstepped their boundaries in suspending Rodriguez for 211 games, and are appealing the suspension.

2.   *Major League Baseball and the Yankees have conspired to force Rodriguez from baseball.*

3.   *The Yankees and the team's doctor have conspired to allow Rodriguez to play with a severe injury, so that he would look terrible playing and also so that he could, possibly, aggravate the injury to the point where he could no longer play.*

4.   *The Yankees' President told the team doctor that it would not be a problem if Rodriguez's surgery last off-season rendered him unable to play.*

5.   *Rodriguez is planning on bringing litigation against the team's doctor for hiding the true nature and extent of A-Rod's hip injury.*

So realistically, what more can Rodriguez or his legal team even say?

At the same time, pronouncing a vow of media silence permits Rodriguez and his counsel to dodge the big question, the one asked by Matt Lauer of attorney Joe Tacopina last week – *why not agree with Major League Baseball's proposal to publicly reveal all of the evidence that MLB has against Rodriguez and Rodriguez has against MLB and the Yankees?* There is little doubt that exposure of the evidence would work against Rodriguez. By instituting a bogus "vow of silence" Rodriguez and his attorneys have given themselves the best chance of skirting the issue, while all of their allegations hang in the air like balloons ready to explode over the heads of the Lords of Baseball and the Yankee brass.

Here's the reality - **Rodriguez has not instructed his counsel to do or not to do anything**. Rodriguez's counsel has come to the realization that their media blitzkrieg has reached its apex, and that any further comments can only do more harm than good. **Counsel has advised Rodriguez that the media battle must now cease,** and has instructed him to make the proclamation to the media that he, somehow, is the one who is calling the shots for "Team A-Rod."

And the media, somehow and inexplicably believing Rodriguez, has accepted his comments and reported them without question. A bunch of maroons, indeed.

Extra Innings: This time, I wasn't kidding, despite the Bugs Bunny reference.

Eventually, all of the lawsuits were dismissed and Alex began to toe the company line. Always in the headlines, however, he then had a mini-spat with his then-former attorney. By the time 2015 rolled around, however, Rodriguez morphed into a model employee and somehow was able to keep himself in check for the entire season.

Thank God for A-Rod, All of You Ballplayers

(Originally posted January 12, 2014)

It turns out that Alex Rodriguez has been lying to us the whole time. Despite his contentions that he has been telling the truth through what he has termed the "ordeal" surrounding the allegations and suspension due to his use of performance-enhancing drugs, his statement in response to the Arbitrator's decision, issued yesterday, clearly indicates that he has been pulling the wool over our eyes since day one – at least as to his intentions and concerns, that is.

Initially, we thought that his fight against the allegations and suspension was all about Alex. This was a fair assumption since, to be honest, everything has been about Alex since he first donned a baseball uniform, every move calculated to cultivate a certain mystique and persona. Then, halfway through this ordeal, he switched gears and made it about his children, and about how they would perceive their father and his legacy.

Now, however, Alex has finally revealed his true intentions, his true concerns. And we were all wrong about him. Completely wrong. This is not a fight to save Alex's career and allow him to continue to bulk up his statistics, so that he can one day retire as the major league leader in every power/offensive category. We were obviously oversimplifying things when we believed that to be true. And for that, I think, we all owe A-Rod a tremendous apology.

Because now we know the real root of his concerns – the continued welfare and well-being of - get this - **every other major league player**! It never occurred to me, nor, it appears anyone else, that the man whom we all thought was completely selfish was actually playing the role of savior for his brethren, to protect their futures at his own expense!! In case you missed his statement from yesterday, here is the proof. The statement reads, in relevant part:

81

BLOGGIN' BASEBALL II (FROM THE BLEACHERS) - ANDREW WOLFENSON

"...This injustice is MLB's first step toward abolishing guaranteed contracts in the 2016 bargaining round, instituting lifetime bans for single violations of drug policy, and further insulating its corrupt investigative program from any variety defense by accused players, or any variety of objective review...

No player should have to go through what I have been dealing with, and I am exhausting all options to ensure not only that I get justice, but that players' contracts and rights are protected through the next round of bargaining, and that the MLB investigation and arbitration process cannot be used against others in the future the way it is currently being used to unjustly punish me."

Reading it again brings a tear to my eye. Alex Rodriguez is not selfish. Alex Rodriguez is, dare I say, the Mother Teresa of major league baseball players. He is exactly the opposite of the selfish, me-first, preening ballplayer – he is putting the interests of everyone else before his! "Suspend me, and that's OK," he seems to be saying, "but I will not let you abolish guaranteed contracts for my fellow players, I will not let you have any tainted investigations against my brothers on the diamond, and you will not be able to, under any circumstances, violate the rights of my fellow players, my brothers *(insert tear here)* because I will not let you!" Alex Rodriguez is not selfish, people; rather, Alex Rodriguez is SELFLESS!

And he is doing it alone, which makes it even more remarkable and heroic. While Alex is threatening to head to Federal Court tomorrow in an attempt to obtain an injunction against the suspension – presumably, based on his statements above, to show the bullies at Major League Baseball that they can't keep any player down – Solidarity!! – and not just to allow him to continue to play and amass more possibly steroid-fueled statistics, the MLB Player's Association, the very union constructed to protect these players, is not going along for the ride. The statement issued by the Player's Association reads, in part, as follows:

"While we respectfully disagree with the Arbitrator's ruling, we will abide by it as we continue to vigorously challenge Alex's suspension within the context of this hearing."

So the players' own labor union will continue to challenge the suspension, but only "within the context of this hearing." Not in court. Only within the confines of the arbitration hearing which resulted in the issuance of the 162-game suspension. Is it any wonder, then, that the players need someone like Alex to rise above the concerns for his own welfare and to take the appropriate action to defend their rights?

All of the players, clearly, should be thanking God for A-Rod.

Let's see what happens tomorrow when he tries to go to court to protect his fellow players. It will also be interesting to hear what Tony Bosch has to say on tonight's *60 Minutes*, because the snippets played on CBS yesterday appear to indicate that Alex did, in fact, take various forms of steroids or PED's, which means that he is also lying when he denies doing so. Maybe we just can't trust him. Ask Katie Couric. He lied to her in a televised interview years ago. There seems to be a pattern developing …

Extra Innings: When he did return to the Yankees in 2015, Rodriguez clearly did so with the assistance of a media consultant. He said all of the right things about being thankful for the opportunity to play again, about being a team player, etc. In fact, everything he said during the 2015 season was perfect, until his proclamation that "we play for CC" after CC Sabathia entered alcohol rehabilitation on the eve of the Yankees' Wild Card playoff game against Houston. Rodriguez went 0-4 in that game with two strikeouts.

Baseball Vigilantes? Better Watch Out, A-Rod

(Originally posted January 22, 2014)

The Major League Baseball Player's Association has sent a clear message to Alex Rodriguez – that they no longer want him as a member and will take matters into their own hands should he decide to step back onto a baseball diamond in 2015, after he serves his 162-game suspension for using performance enhancing drugs and hindering baseball's investigation into such usage. The Union had backed A-Rod's appeal of his suspension up until the time that the arbitration panel shaved his unplanned vacation to 162 games – essentially the 2014 season, but its support of Alex ended when Rodriguez made the ill-fated decision, along with his cadre of counsel, to bring litigation against not only Major League Baseball, but also his own union.

His allegations that the union and its former head, the late (and beloved) Michael Weiner, did not adequately protect him were met, predictably, with hostility. According to reports, during a recent conference call, one player asked to have A-Rod kicked out of the union. Not one person disagreed with this action, although union leaders advised that they could not do so. At least one player, however, said that A-Rod would be little more than a target for pitchers should he enter the batter's box.

As one player allegedly said, according to www.foxsports.com, "[w]hen he gets up to bat, you can hit him and hit him hard … That's what I'd do. He sued us. Jhonny Peralta and Nelson Cruz screwed up. You know what? They owned up to it. They took their medicine … [Rodriguez] needs to be scared of coming back and facing people he sued. If he can't fear the wrath of getting kicked out or not being included, he's going to be forced out."

*****

85

I can't avoid noting at least a little comedy in the above statement. Peralta and Cruz "took their medicine"? Yes, they were each suspended for 50 games – but, really, at what cost? Peralta signed a contract with St. Louis during the off-season which will pay him the princely sum of $53 million over the next four years. Maybe some of us can endure the "bitter taste" of such medicine. And his new teammate, Matt Holliday, apparently said the following just two days ago, according to ESPN, "I am against PEDs and always will be. But I also am a forgiving person, and he served his suspension. That's the rules of the game. I'm happy to have him as a teammate." Yet again, I would urge, we are shown that the ramifications of taking PEDs are minimal at best – so why should players comply with the rules? They may get suspended, but then they are rewarded with multi-million dollar contracts and the forgiveness of their new teammates. Seems like a pretty good deal to me.

Meanwhile, Cruz is still searching for his payday, but the main reason does not appear to be his drug use. As reported on www.sbnation.com (citing Nick Cafardo of the Boston Globe): "The chances of Cruz, 33, signing a multi-year contract have been hampered by his own refusal to stray far from his earlier contract demands. At the outset of free agency, he made it known that he was looking for a four-year deal worth $75 million ... Also hurting Cruz's chances at a big payday is the fact that he will cost a draft pick to sign ... As has been seen since the advent of the qualifying offer system, teams have been wary to give up picks for non-superstar players ..."

So, it appears, he is not being signed because he asked for too much money and teams don't want to give up a draft pick – not because his statistics may have been faked through his use of steroids.

*****

Back to Alex. How comical would be it to see him step onto the field, for his first at-bat of 2015, as the Yankees' designated hitter? The first pitch thrown to him is clearly aimed at his head, and he steps forward, jawing at the pitcher for throwing at him. The opposing team's dugout empties, and two dozen enemy ballplayers swarm onto the field. The Yankees, meanwhile, stay seated in the dugout and bullpen, none of them willing to enter the field to protect their teammate. All except the Yankees' union player representative (whomever that will be, as it used to be Curtis Granderson, now with the Mets). That guy leaps from the dugout and wraps his arms around Rodriguez, presumably to restrain him from going after the pitcher. In doing so, however, he sucker punches his teammate, and then holds him up while the opposing players take their turn pounding him to the turf.

It won't happen, of course. The tenor of these statements, which are likely to continue should Alex continue his litigious ways, will not change. Even the narcissistic A-Rod may see that his time on the diamond has expired, and will simply seek a buyout of his contract with the Yankees and call it a career. That will be his version of "taking his medicine", I suppose. To the tune of $61 million.

Where do we sign up for that? I don't even care if that medicine is covered by insurance.

Extra Innings: Rodriguez returned to the Yankees in 2015 and walloped 33 home runs. There were no clear incidents of his being targeted by opposing pitchers. He is set to return to the Yankees in 2016.

CHAPTER 3 – STEROIDS AND PED'S

The Allure of Money, Not PED's, Is Baseball's Real Disease

(Originally posted June 5, 2013)

"I've been in minor league and major league clubhouses ... I know the pressures and what goes on ... it is coming from the perspective of a guy who had to fight for everything I got in the big leagues ...

I saw what kind of money it is going to get you. I had great minor league seasons, but I wanted to stay in the big leagues. I know my teammates and I know guys on other teams are doing it, and they're hitting home runs left and right. And I'm sitting there going, 'All right, well, what I'm going to do?'"

-    *Shane Monahan, former outfielder, Seattle Mariners (1998-1999)*

According to Major League Baseball, Anthony Bosch is ready to cooperate. The Director of Biogenesis, a Florida anti-aging clinic, is now ready to speak with baseball's representatives and, in so doing, will likely implicate almost two dozen baseball players in the latest MLB performance enhancing drug scandal. Reports indicate that suspensions are likely to be handed down as a result of the ongoing investigation, including two of the game's biggest stars, Alex Rodriguez and Ryan Braun.

This is merely the latest black mark on the National Pastime and the latest example of its continued failure to properly exorcise the sport of those who utilize performance enhancing substances. While it would be imprudent to automatically assume that all of the players named in the Biogenesis ledgers actually did use some form of illegal or improper substances, it would also be naïve to assume that all of the named players are innocent. Several of the players named in the report, including Rodriguez, Bartolo Colon, and Melky Cabrera, have already admitted to using illegal substances or have previously been suspended by the MLB for their usage of such drugs.

I could step on my soapbox now and condemn the players who have used illegal drugs and who have steadfastly lied about such usage, but I have already done that.

I could wax poetic about the players involved in this scandal and refer back to the famous steroid users of the past, like Mark McGwire and Roger Clemens, but I have already done that.

Or, I could bemoan the fact that Braun's continued inclusion in the Biogenesis scandal bothers me greatly as it will potentially undermine the achievements of one of the best Jewish baseball players ever to step onto a baseball diamond. Again, however, I have already done that.

In reality, however, baseball's continued attacks on steroids and other PED's is little more than trying to attack the manifestations of a disease, and not the disease itself. And continuing to proceed in this manner will never cure the sport of its ills. There will be periodic band-aids and temporary elixirs, at least publically, but the underlying disease remains – and as long as it remains, there will be players who will find new ways to stay one step ahead of the various cures, potions, and vaccines – at least until they are caught.

The disease, of course, is money. The allure of making millions of dollars is simply too great for these players to pass up; and it is difficult, when you think about it, to condemn them for trying to get a competitive edge when obtaining such an edge can be so lucrative. In 2012, the average salary for a major league baseball player was $3,200,000. The minimum salary for a major league baseball player in 2013 is $490,000. That means that the last player on a team, the player who may see only action once a week, if not less, will make almost a half a million dollars per year. That may seem like a paltry amount when compared to the millionaires with whom he will share the locker room, but it is still far greater than the overwhelming majority of the fans cheering for the team will make this year.

Reading Shane Monahan's quotes above should be chilling to the lords of baseball, who continue to shell out untold amounts of money to men and boys for playing a game, many of whom come from middle- and lower-class backgrounds and who could never replicate, or even approach the vicinity, of their salary ranges. And like the sirens of ancient mythology, the allure of the big bucks makes some (likely most) of the players do what they can, even if improper, to ensure their position on a major league roster and guarantee their hefty paychecks.

Does it pay off for the players? It certainly seems so in certain instances. Take, for example, Melky Cabrera. Prior to 2011, Melky had never hit for higher than a .274 batting average in any season. From 2010 through 2012, his average increased seemingly exponentially, from .255 in 2010 to .305 in 2011 to .346 in 2012. From 2010 to 2011, his home runs went from 4 to 18, both his RBI's and runs scored increased over 100%, and he stole three times as many bases. In 2012, his OPS (on-base % plus slugging %) increased almost 100 points. Then, however, the bottom fell out – he was suspended for the last 49 games of the 2012 season due to the steroid allegations. One would think that such a tainted player, even one who was leading the National League in batting average with a gaudy .346 when he was suspended, would be a pariah and would have trouble finding a new team for 2013.

One would, however, be incorrect. Melky not only found a new team, but signed for a cool $16 million dollars over two years – meaning that his drug usage was rewarded to the tune of $8 million dollars per year. And his statistics this year seem to belie a player who is no longer "on the juice" as his numbers are sharply down from last season's. As of today, he has played 58 games this season, approximately half of the number of games last season – so, one would assume that his numbers this year would be about half of last year's, right? Again, however, such an assumption would be incorrect. First, the batting average – last year .346 and leading the league, this year a more pedestrian .284 – not bad, but his lowest since 2010. He has only 24 runs scored, far less than half of the 84 that he tallied last year, and he has only two home runs and two triples, far less than the eleven and ten that he tallied, respectively, in 2012. His total of 60 RBI's last season has plummeted to 21, and his 13 stolen bases of last year have been replaced with a paltry two swipes in 2013. His OPS has dropped like a stone, from .906 to .703. What these numbers show, clearly, is a player whose skills are either declining (but he is only 28 years old) or a player who is simply not performing at the level that he had in the past – which begs the question of why? Lack of PED use is the obvious reason, of course, which leads to the next question – why would a team shell out so much money for a player whose performance could have been expected to decline dramatically if he were to "be clean" of such PED use?

Another member of the Biogenesis accused is Mariners' catcher Jesus Montero. Once hailed as the Yankees' "catcher of the future," Montero made an immediate impact with the Bronx Bombers in 2011 as a 21-year old rookie, slugging four home runs and batting .328 in only 18 big-league games. To the chagrin of the Yankee faithful, he was traded that off-season to Seattle, and responded to his new surroundings by belting 15 home runs and 20 doubles in 2012. Despite high hopes this season, through 29 games played in 2013 he had hit only three home runs and had only nine RBI's to go along with his pitiful .208 batting average; numbers which earned him a ticket to the minor leagues.

Can it be that his numbers decreased so dramatically this season because he stopped using PED's? Of course it is possible; I do not profess to know if this is true or not, but certainly the numbers and his appearance in the Biogenesis ledgers properly raise the question.

*****

So if money is the disease, then what can be done to eradicate the use of PED's in baseball?

Likely nothing. As long as you have boys who live in poverty, whether in this country, Latin America, or otherwise, and have an ability to either throw or hit a ball better than anyone else in their hometown, there will be PED use. When a boy sets on a course from a young age to play in the majors, playing every day after school, forsaking other activities and, often, forsaking studying or even attending school in order to achieve his dream of playing, then, when he becomes a man and has no other appreciable skills, how can we expect him to simply accept being a career minor-leaguer, or being shut out from the game he loves, if his skills are only slightly lesser than others? Can we blame the player for seeking that edge, like Shane Monahan and so many like him?

Perhaps it is time for baseball to either institute a salary cap and allow for more reasonable salaries, or just accept the reality that its players can use PEDs, as long as they are not illegal substances. While this would be difficult to monitor properly, if all players are permitted to use the PEDs, then they will all still be on a level playing field. Yes, it would send a bad message to America's youth; but accepting the reality may be better in the long run for the game – because so long as the allure of the money remains, as long as the siren's song resonates in terms of millions of dollars, there will be players like Alex Rodriguez who seek to somehow justify a $30 million dollar per year contract, and, more often, players like Shane Monahan who seek their smaller piece of the pie that is a major league salary, whether the average salary of $3,200,000 or the minimum salary of $490,000.

Honestly, I could see myself taking some HGH if it meant making that kind of money for a brief, five-year career in the majors. I could start at the $490,000, work my way to $750,000 the next year, and then get, say, $2 million for the next two years and then get to the average of $3.2 million, all for being a journeyman infielder or left-handed relief pitcher. That would allow me to earn $8.44 million dollars over five years, certainly enough to allow me to pursue other avenues of employment thereafter without the need of worrying about whether or not my retirement or my children's educations were properly funded. How can I expect baseball players to think any differently?

Extra Innings: It is really painfully obvious. Rumors abound, meanwhile, that players are still using PED's and other substances, but they are just getting better at hiding the usage. It would be hard to believe that this is not the case. I put it this way – if someone asked me to fudge the numbers on a real estate closing and that they would pay me double my normal fee for a closing, I would tell them to get out of my office. If, however, someone told me that if I fudged the numbers on a real estate closing they would give me $10 million, and that I would only have to serve a one-year suspension if I were to get caught, and then I would be able to come back and practice law without any decrease in my business, well, let's be real. Where do I sign up?

Former MVP Ryan Braun Suspended - Who Will Agree to Be Next?

(Originally posted July 23, 2013)

Ryan Braun, Brewers' slugger and former National League MVP, has accepted a 65-game suspension from Major League Baseball. The suspension essentially ends his 2013 season, as well as that of his team. Braun will not be paid during this suspension, which softens the blow to a team which is already mired in last place – that part of his salary which will be retained by the team will no doubt work as a decent set-off to the decreased attendance which will result from his absence.

The suspension of Braun, and his tacit admission (*he admits that he has made "mistakes" and that he is "not perfect"*) that he has used Performance Enhancing Drugs, underscore a watershed moment in baseball's latest war against steroids and other PED's. I could write a post about how the fall from grace of the man known as "The Hebrew Hammer" is troubling to the Jewish community due to his stature as one of its previously-shining lights, but I have already done that.

I could write about how this is a rare example of how baseball has singled out one of its "good guys" and that making Braun the first casualty of the Biogenesis probe is shocking in that the league did not first suspend one of the lesser-loved performers, such as the polarizing Alex Rodriguez. I have previously addressed the "good guy v. bad guy" theory as well.

Instead, however, this post will focus on the fact that Braun immediately accepted his suspension when it was announced by MLB, which leads to the inescapable conclusion that it was negotiated between the parties. One cannot help but think that Braun's almost two years of defiance and self-righteous denials of PED use simply could not be erased overnight. Since he was first accused of using PED's following his 2011 MVP campaign, Braun has consistently maintained his innocence. Even when he was cleared of such use based on little more than a technicality when his urine sample was mishandled in the past, he steadfastly denied using any improper substances. Even though his image was slightly tarnished and his smile turned to a steely grimace by his constant denials, he still remained as a "positive" force in the league and, until the Biogenesis information was leaked, seemed to have survived the initial round of suspicion. So why change his tune now? Why would the player's union allow him to accept the suspension without filing an appeal or grievance?

The only answer is that the unpaid and unplanned vacation was negotiated. We do not know for how long these negotiations have been on-going, but the fact that the first player suspended was a former MVP (the first former MVP to receive such a suspension) and that it is effective immediately, rather than next year, is quite surprising in light of the recent stories from baseball "insiders" and pundits who proclaimed that no action would be effective until at least the beginning of the 2014 season. Perhaps the fact that the Brewers' season is, for all intents and purposes, already over contributed to the decision to suspend Braun now, rather than the beginning of 2014 when the Brewers might have had an opportunity to earn a playoff berth.

The natural question now, of course, is which players will be next? Logic dictates that if the league is willing to suspend Braun, then *no player*, irrespective of his importance or value to his team, will be impervious to suspension. The obvious choice to fall next, to many, will be Alex Rodriguez. Certainly the evidence that the league had against Braun could not have exceeded the presumed mountain of paperwork that it must have against Rodriguez, right? So, some may argue, Rodriguez should now be worried that a suspension is in his future. But to take this position may be to ignore what is likely going on behind the scenes …

The use of steroids and PED's has remained a festering sore spot on major league baseball. Suspensions add to the embarrassment. They are made much worse when the players and/or the Players' Association appeal, creating a circus-like atmosphere which further alienates the game from its fan base. So negotiating the suspensions, with the understanding that they will not be appealed, makes perfect sense from a business standpoint.

Having said that, it is not beyond the realm of possibility that negotiations have been ongoing with some of the other targets of the Biogenesis investigation, including two players who were suspended last year, Bartolo Colon and Melky Cabrera, as well as the afore-mentioned Mr. A-Rod. Of these three, the loss of Colon, at this time, would prove to be the most damaging to his team – the A's are currently sitting atop the American League West, three games above the Texas Rangers (who have their own target in slugger Nelson Cruz), and the loss of Colon, who currently sports a 13-3 won-loss record to go with his microscopic 2.52 ERA, would be crippling to the youthful Oakland squad. A-Rod or Cabrera would seem to be the next likely sacrificial lamb based on their team's relative positions in the standings, although the New York media has been all but gushing over Rodriguez lately as his possible return to the Yankees from hip surgery approached.

What Major League Baseball has done through the arranged suspension of Braun, however, is set itself in position to take strong stances against the other players, should they not agree to "play ball" with the league as far as taking their own unpaid vacations from the field. Jettisoning a former MVP from his team is as strong a message as the league could send, and there is little doubt that it was contrived as such. Publicly, the players are saying that they want the game cleaned up. By making Braun the first casualty of this scandal, it appears that the league is heeding the players' call. The only question now is how many other players are willing to fall on their bats (or gloves) to further the game's purpose, at their own personal expense – both with respect to income and popularity, or whether the rest of the accused are simply suspended by the league without their consent, which will lead to inevitable appeals and grievances being filed.

Arguably the biggest player involved has been removed from the game. Now, the others should fall like dominoes, perhaps within the next few days or so – and it will be interesting to see how the Players' Association reacts, now that it has not intervened on Braun's behalf. It will also be interesting to see how the public reacts when the suspensions are real, and not theoretical, and whether people will continue to visit ballparks in the cities where stars have been placed on hiatus, especially where the players' suspensions can have a detrimental effect on their teams' ability to compete.

Extra Innings: **After Braun, another dozen players accepted suspensions for the remainder of the 2013 season. The only suspended player who put up a fuss was Alex Rodriguez, who instituted various lawsuits, naming as defendants Major League Baseball, the Yankees, the Players' Union, and his doctor. Rodriguez eventually sat out (involuntarily) the entire 2014 season, and returned to the Yankees for the 2015 season.**

A Moment of Sanity in Baseball's Steroid Controversy?

(Originally posted August 11, 2013)

Is it possible that the baseball-related "steroids lynch mob" has at least a semblance of sanity? This week, former Giants' and Cardinals' slugger Jack Clark, who was recently hired as a radio talk show host in St. Louis, attempted to "out" former St. Louis superstar Albert Pujols as a steroid user. According to Clark, when he was the hitting coach for the Los Angeles Dodgers over a decade ago, he was told by the team's conditioning coach that the latter had "shot" Pujols with steroids, and that he (Clark) should try the same to get into better condition. Clark detailed a conversation with the conditioning coach, Chris Mihlfeld, where he claims that Mihlfeld told him that Pujols had been juicing since college - as Clark recounted, Mihlfeld told him that he had been working out with Pujols – *"threw him batting practice, worked him out, shot him up, all that stuff."*

Out in California, the story got press – Pujols is, after all, currently sitting on an albatross of a contract that he signed with the Anaheim-based Angels. The 10-year deal will pay Pujols a total of $240 million dollars, and the production that the team has received thus far from the former Cardinals' star has been significantly less than expected – this season's numbers include only 17 home runs and 64 RBI's to go along with his .258 batting average; decent statistics, but not when compared to his first dozen seasons and not sufficient to warrant a $24 million payday each year. In fact, his reduction in production is just the type of statistical malaise that people point to when they want to show that someone who *was* taking steroids *is now* off of the juice – although he was starting to show increased production before being sidelined with a partial tear of his plantar fascia.

It seems in this case that Clark has overplayed his hand in a valiant attempt to increase ratings and somehow make himself relevant again. Pujols immediately threatened to sue Clark and his radio employer for what he characterized as Clark's lies – and Clark reportedly has been fired from his gig, only one week into his new career. It did not help Clark that he also accused current Tigers' ace Justin Verlander of using steroids as well, without any "proof" other than what he perceived to be Verlander's drop in production and pitch velocity in 2013. Also, Mihlfeld immediately rebuked Clark's statements, telling ESPN.com that *"I haven't even talked to Jack Clark in close to 10 years ... His statements are simply not true. I have known Albert Pujols since he was 18 years old, and he would never use illegal drugs in any way... both Albert and I have been accused of something we didn't do."*

*****

Some media outlets seemingly did not even feel the need to justify Clark's comments with a story – Saturday's *Star-Ledger*, for example, made no mention of either Clark's accusations or Pujols' denials. Apparently the continuing Alex Rodriguez soap opera is enough PED news for now here on the East Coast – A-Rod was booed by most fans during his return to da Bronx Friday night, especially after he struck out three times and was hitless in four at-bats; despite the boo birds and "Bronx cheers", however, Rodriguez – continuing to live in a state of complete denial – stated, according to ESPNNewYork.com, that *"[i]t was awesome, it was an amazing experience . The fans were incredible. Such great energy and such a great response. It was pretty overwhelming. I was having a hard time keeping my emotions in check."*

*****

Note that this is not the first time that Pujols has been accused of using steroids – frankly, any slugger of this era is subject to suspicion, and Albert's eleven straight years of 30 or more homers and ten straight seasons of 100+ RBIs (he had 99 in the eleventh) while in St. Louis opened him up to a great deal of chatter, more like questions, about how he could be so successful. A Rookie of the Year award, three MVP awards, and nine All-Star game appearances in a

102

Cardinals' uniform also made him quite the target – much like another three-time MVP award winner who consistently amassed statistics which included 30+ home runs and 100+ RBI's per year –Alex Rodriguez.

The difference, however, is that although Pujols could be surly at times and, he has not been and will never be the villain that Rodriguez has become. To the contrary, he was signed by Anaheim not only for his slugging ability, but also to be a positive Hispanic face for a franchise seeking to increase its Latino fan base, according to numerous reports at the time of his signing. Also, including Verlander in his comments, without any basis whatsoever, immediately called Clark's credibility into question – unlike Rodriguez, who has previously admitted the use of PED's and who was swept up in the massive Biogenesis scandal, along with at least 16 other players who have previously served or who are currently serving suspensions for their PED usage.

Pujols' statement, released Friday, read, in part, as follows: *"I am going to send a message that you cannot act in a reckless manner, like [Clark has], and get away with it. If I have to be the athlete to carry the torch and pave the way for other innocent players to see that you can do something about it, I am proud to be that person. I have five young children and I take being a role model very seriously. The last thing I want is for the fans, and especially the kids out there, to question my reputation and character."*

Interestingly, this was delivered only a scant week after A-Rod made a similar statement about being a role model, but when A-Rod made the comment, everyone snickered. Here, people seem to be taking Albert seriously. It is a self-serving comment, to be certain, and is no less self-serving than the denial issued by Mihlfeld, who was previously linked to at least one player, Jason Grimsley, who admitted to the use of PED's and was suspended in 2006.

For some reason, however, perhaps due to the ferocity of the denials, it appears, for now, that Pujols has the upper hand. There is simply no valid reason for Clark to make allegations about an alleged discussion from the turn of the century – unless, of course, to draw more attention to his radio show – which makes his, perhaps, the most self-serving comments of all.

In a Major League career that spanned 18 years, Jack Clark appeared in four All-Star games, finished in the Top 10 four times in MVP balloting, and slugged 340 homers. He also struck out 1,441 times in his career, however – but at no time, it seems, did he whiff as greatly as he did with his ill-timed and ill-advised (and, possibly, incorrect) comments about Albert Pujols.

Extra Innings: This proved to be, at least according to the Open Salon website, my most widely-read blog post. According to the site, this post was viewed 70,698 times as of March 23, 2015, just before the whole place was shut down.

There have been no more rumors regarding Albert Pujols and alleged steroid use.

Jason Giambi Feels Loved In Cleveland; Steroids? Who, Him?

(Originally posted September 25, 2013)

… so is there hope for Alex Rodriguez??

Before the Biogenesis scandal rocked Major League Baseball last year, there was BALCO. The Bay Area Laboratory Co-Operative was the previously-best known supplier of steroids and other Performance Enhancing Drugs to baseball players, and stars like all-time Home Run king Barry Bonds and Gary Sheffield were swept up in the investigation of the company's practices.

As was Jason Giambi. At the time, Giambi was a hulking, mountain of a man, a slugger imported to the Bronx by the Yankees from his prior position in Oakland by a siren which took the form of an equally giant, seven-year, $120 million contract after the 2001 season. Between 1998 and 2003, he crushed 223 Home Runs, was named to five All-Star teams, and he won the MVP award in 2000. And then it call came crashing down for the man known as the "Giambino," when the steroid allegations, and thinly-veiled admissions, brought an inglorious end to his time in New York.

Giambi has bounced around since then, spending time in Oakland, Colorado, and now with the upstart Indians.

Last night, the 42-year old Giambi stroked what may be the biggest hit of his career – a walk-off, two-run home run which lifted the Indians to a 5-4 victory and kept them one game ahead of the Texas Rangers in the fight for the last wild-card spot in this year's playoffs. After the game, manager Terry Francona admitted that he has a "man crush" on Giambi, and no doubt many of his teammates and the Indians' fans share his love of the aging slugger.

His story is reminiscent of another former MVP winner and perennial All-Star, a man who has smashed hundreds of steroid-fueled home runs. So will the future contain a similar, positive twist of fate for the beleaguered A-Rod? Will a future Yankees' manager and the Bronx faithful confess to having "Man crushes" on an older, presumably wiser Alex Rodriguez?

Only time will tell. Here's hoping not, however.

Extra Innings: Shockingly, at least to this writer, it was the Bronx fans who quickly developed man crushes on Alex. Once the season began and he started hitting the ball, it seemed as if his past transgressions vanished into thin air. Being a sports fan, for some (if not most) truly is a "what have you done for me lately" mentality.

Barry Bonds Tries to Upstage the World Series, But Fails

(Originally posted October 29, 2013)

Last night, the Crimson Stockings from Beantown defeated the Cardinals and moved to within one win of capturing their third World Series championship in ten years. More importantly for Red Sox Nation, the team stands on the verge of winning their first title at home, in cozy and historic Fenway Park, for the first time in 95 years. For some, this is cause for great celebration. For others, watching the Sox move to the precipice of baseball nirvana again has left us with the taste of bile in our mouths.

The disgust over the on-the-field events, however, should actually pale in comparison to the off-the-field shenanigans. The Alex Rodriguez fiasco continues both in the land of Arbitration and the Federal Court system, albeit quietly during the last week. Just as the media attention over Alex and his gang of counsel, including battling Joe Tacopina, has died down, however, today's paper contains mention of another tainted slugger wasting the court's time and resources.

From today's *Newark Star Ledger*:

"Major League Baseball's all-time home run leader has asked a federal appeals court to reconsider its refusal of overturn his felony obstruction conviction.

Barry Bonds' legal team filed the request yesterday with the 9th U.S. Circuit Court of Appeals in San Francisco. A three-judge panel of the 9th Circuit upheld Bonds' conviction in September.

A jury found him guilty in April 2011. Bonds is asking the court to assemble a special panel of 11 judges to rehear the case.

Bonds argues that he was wrongfully convicted of obstruction of justice for giving a rambling but truthful answer during a 2003 grand jury appearance.

Bonds was asked whether his trainer had injected him with a substance, and he replied by discussing the difficulties of being the son of a famous father."

107

<u>Eleven Judges?</u>

Bonds wants a panel of eleven judges convened to hear his case. Eleven! What a complete waste of taxpayer money that would be. Perhaps Mr. Bonds does not read the newspapers. Perhaps he knows nothing of our recent government shutdown, and nothing of our continued economic woes. Clearly, he does not realize that those eleven judges are on the public payroll and that taking the time to hear his appeal will thereby take them away from other courtrooms and dealing with other cases in the already backlogged system, right?

Wrong. He knows. He just does not care. To him, it always has been and always will be all about Barry.

<u>Let's Be Realistic – He is Guilty of Something</u>

Al Capone went to jail for tax evasion, not for his "gangster" activities. OJ Simpson went to jail for false imprisonment of someone in a hotel room, not for killing his ex-wife. Each was convicted of something, if for no other reason than that they were guilty of something else. The feds could not get Capone on the other charges, so the tax evasion charges led to jail. OJ was famously and inexplicably found not guilty of murdering his ex-wife and Ron Goldman, but the later trial in Vegas ended in conviction, in what is known on the gridiron or baseball diamond as a "make-up call."

Bonds clearly was guilty of taking steroids in violation of baseball rules. He then clearly lied about it, and continues to lie about it. He does admit to taking the substances (known as the "cream" and the "clear") but says that he did not know that these substances were steroids. Really? This clearly defies all logic, as it has with other baseball stars who gave similar denials. Here's the reality – if you are a professional athlete, making millions upon millions of dollars, you no doubt monitor everything that goes into your body, for at least two reasons – one, to

108

avoid getting in trouble and two, more importantly, so that you don't cause your body harm and lose the ability to make the millions of dollars. Barry Bonds clearly knew what he was doing, and yet has denied, denied, denied it. If the worst the Feds could do to him was catch him on that stupid question, then so be it.

Yes, I am forgetting what I do for a living for the purposes of this post. Common sense takes over sometimes – and this is one of those times. The guy is guilty. Guilty of something. If this is where the record will prove him so, then so be it. He is not rehabilitating his image, and it's not like he cannot get a new job because he has a record. This is all about ego. The court system cannot continue to feed it.

The Timing of the Filing

Disclosure – I do not know if the papers had to be filed yesterday, or if counsel had some type of deadline to meet. In light of the fact that nothing has seemingly taken place in the Bonds case for so long, however, I find it difficult to believe that there was such an urgency to filing and, rather, it appears that same was timed to be done during the World Series for maximum exposure and to detract, quite selfishly, from the teams currently vying for the title. That plan seems to have failed, however, as the article in today's *Star Ledger*, quoted in its entirety above, was relegated to the bottom of the second page of the sports section. This is clearly not the media splash that Bonds' counsel was seeking. That it did not garner more attention (I know, a bit cynical in light of this post) is a good thing.

Partners in Crime

Boston's David Ortiz now has eleven hits in the first five games in this year's World Series. Along with his four walks, that means that he has reached base 15 times in the five games. The only other player to accomplish this feat? The afore-mentioned Barry Bonds, in 2002. That gives the men three things in common – you know, along with using steroids and lying about it.

Wasting the Government's Resources

Bonds' filing goes to prove, to a certain extent, one of the differences between the "haves" and "have-nots" of our society: that those with unlimited funds can continue to meander their way through the legal system time and again in an attempt to get the result they want. It is reminiscent of when OJ was first accused – there was an attorney being interviewed on television who spoke at length about the steps he would take to defend OJ. When asked if he would expend such resources on a different client, like someone less wealthy than OJ (meaning almost everyone) the attorney was speechless. Clearly he would not have done so, but OJ's money made all things possible – case in point – it made the Kardashian family famous – so, in a way, we are still all paying for OJ's sins.

Bonds made millions of dollars swinging the bat and hitting home runs. Many of those dollars appear to have been ill-gotten, as they resulted from his steroid-enhanced performance and his increased ability to "cream" the balls as they approached the plate. Now, he is using many of those dollars in an attempt to "clear" his name even though such exoneration is not warranted.

*****

In a nutshell, here's the skinny – Barry Bonds fooled the American public for years into thinking that his ability to stroke a baseball was legitimate. Then, when he was caught, he tried to fool the public again (and has somehow succeeded in the Bay Area, as I have previously written) by somehow claiming that he did not know what substances he was putting into his body. Now, he is trying to further screw the American public by forcing our government to waste precious judicial and monetary resources fighting, in court, the ridiculous and desperate filings of a guilty party.

Here's hoping that the Court summarily dismisses his petition without a hearing, and, more importantly, without the convening of eleven judges at taxpayer's expense. That way, one of the poster children for Baseball's ills will not be able to lay his steroid-enlarged head on his pillow at night, comforted with the knowledge that he has cleared his name. He's guilty of something, remember.

Extra Innings: The eleven member panel overturned Bonds' conviction for Obstruction of Justice by a 10-1 count.

As it was reported, "a three-judge panel of the appeals court ruled against Bonds, saying factually accurate but misleading testimony can be obstruction of justice. But the full court then granted a rehearing, and the larger panel ruled Wednesday that Bonds' answers, even if evasive, were not 'material,' or relevant to the criminal investigation.

"Bonds' answer 'says absolutely nothing pertinent to the subject of the grand jury's investigation' and could not have diverted prosecutors or influenced the decision on whether to indict anyone, Judge **Alex Kozinski** said in an opinion joined by four other judges. If Bonds' answer was unclear, Kozinski said, it was up to the prosecutor to clarify it." SF Gate.com. April 23, 2015

The Hypocrisy of Baseball - Cheating Keeps Paying Dividends

(Originally posted November 25, 2013)

Yet again, we are confronted with proof of the hypocrisy of Major League Baseball, a group that will formulate a position, and then stand behind that position, at least until it decides not to stand there anymore. Publically, the lords of baseball are waging a war with steroids and other performance-enhancing drugs. The sport suspended over a dozen players last year for using such illicit substances, and is currently mired in a circus masquerading as an Arbitration hearing over the alleged and continuous drug use of Alex Rodriguez.

But lest we think that the league and its teams are *really taking a firm stance against those who would use performance-enhancing drugs*, the news out of St. Louis should dispel any notion that those caught using PED's will suffer any form of long-term consequences. In fact, for the second off-season in a row, an accused and suspended PED-user has been rewarded for his syringe-focused activities, rewarded in the best way possible - with a multi-million dollar contract.

Last year, it was Melky Cabrera, who catapulted his infamy from PED suspension to a two year, $16 million contract from Toronto. Yesterday, a new winner of the "needle award" was named - former Detroit shortstop Jhonny Peralta, who was suspended for 50 games last season for PED usage. Peralta's additional penalty for breaking one of the most sacred rules of Major League Baseball? A four-year contract with the National League champion Cardinals worth a reported $52 or so million.

Yes, that is correct - four years, over $50 million. For a player who has 156 homers over eleven seasons, and a pedestrian .268 batting average - accumulated, at least in part, while using PEDs!! So what can the Redbirds expect from a clean version of Peralta? Certainly not $12 million or so worth of annual production.

At least some players still understand. Arizona pitcher Brad Ziegler tweeted the following: "it pays to cheat ... Thanks, owners, for encouraging PED use." And free agent pitcher David Aardsma echoed that sentiment, tweeting "Apparently getting suspended for PED's means you get a raise. What's stopping anyone from doing it?"

Apparently nothing. At least until the owners band together to take a proper stand against the cheaters, not just saying what they think the public wants to hear.

No doubt that would lead to claims of collusion by the players, but that is a far nobler "problem" than being exposed as money-hungry hypocrites, if you ask me.

Extra Innings: The cheaters win. See the comments after the earlier blog about how it is all rooted in money.

CHAPTER 4 – PETE ROSE AND THE HALL OF FAME

Pete Rose Talkin' About Steroids - He Just Doesn't Get It

(Originally posted August 13, 2013)

Pete Rose, baseball's banished "hit king" and suspended gambler, has weighed in on the steroid issue. In pure Pete fashion, it focuses not on Biogenesis, the players involved, or the effect of such steroid use on baseball – rather, the comments focus, of course, on Pete. In an interview for a Pittsburgh radio station yesterday, Pete had this to say:

"I made mistakes. I can't whine about it. I'm the one that messed up and I'm paying the consequences. However, if I am given a second chance, I won't need a third chance. And to be honest with you, I picked the wrong vice. I should have picked alcohol. I should have picked drugs or I should have picked up beating up my wife or girlfriend because if you do those three, you get a second chance. They haven't given too many gamblers a second chance in the world of baseball."

The problem is that Pete has consistently "whined about it" for years now – to anyone who will listen. Here are some indisputable facts about Pete:

1) PETE, WHILE MANAGING THE CINCINNATI REDS, WAS A GAMBLER

2) PETE, WHILE MANAGING THE CINCINNATI REDS, GAMBLED ON HIS OWN TEAM

3) PETE STEADFASTLY DENIED THE ALLEGATIONS OF HIS GAMBLING WHILE HE WAS MANAGING THE REDS

4) ONLY 25 YEARS LATER DID PETE ADMIT TO GAMBLING ON REDS' GAMES WHILE HE WAS MANAGING THE TEAM; AND ONLY AT THAT TIME IN ORDER TO SELL BOOKS

5) PETE VOLUNTARILY ACCEPTED A LIFETIME BAN FROM BASEBALL

In the late '80's, when Pete was placing bets on his own team, such gambling was baseball's biggest sin. The prohibition against gambling was inscribed on the walls of every major league clubhouse. It had been "public enemy one" for the Major Leagues since the 1918 "Black Sox" scandal, when eight members of the Chicago White Sox were suspended (also for life) for throwing the World Series (ironically, to Pete's future employers, the Reds). Among the suspended was "Shoeless" Joe Jackson, a superstar who, like Pete, was not permitted entry into the Hall of Fame despite clearly possessing the credentials for such election.

So Pete was right about one thing - baseball does not give gamblers second chances. But he knew that when he was placing those bets. He knew that when the allegations against him first surfaced. And he knew that when, in 1989, he signed off on his lifetime ban from the game.

The calls to reinstitute Pete are growing louder as time passes. They echo as the Halls of Cooperstown rumble with arguments over whether or not to induct those players who have been accused of using steroids and other PED's, although all of those players, to date, have been denied entry. So shed no tears for poor Pete. He got what he deserved and, more importantly, what he agreed to.

Also, the inclusion of *"beating up my wife or girlfriend"* in his comment? Pure Pete. No class whatsoever.

Extra Innings: Pete's application for reinstatement is under consideration by Commissioner Rob Manfred. The Commissioner has stated that he will rule before the end of 2015.

Are Baseball Hall of Fame Voters Too Sanctimonious?

(Originally posted January 11, 2014)

This week's baseball Hall of Fame vote has, not surprisingly, again stirred up the conflict surrounding the possible election (or, more appropriately, non-election) of those former stars who have been linked to steroid use. Three players who excelled through the heart of baseball's "steroid era" were chosen for enshrinement, all of whom shared one major asset – none was ever, in any way, linked to or accused of using performance-enhancing drugs. The selections of former pitchers Greg Maddux and Tom Glavine, as well as former slugger Frank Thomas, cannot be questioned. All were certainly worthy of induction, and that all made it on their first appearance on the ballot only serves to codify their qualifications for entry. The only real controversy surrounding these three focused on how 16 voters could have left Maddux off of their ballots – but the question of how some idiots continue to adhere to their position that there should never be a unanimous selection is best left for another day.

Rather, there remains a controversy surrounding the non-election of the steroid users and, worse, the alleged steroid users. As any true fan is aware, few of the players currently on the ballot (Mark McGwire, Rafael Palmeiro) ever truly tested positive for steroid use or admitted to taking such substances. One, Bonds, admitted using but claimed that he was unaware of what he was taking. Others have been suspected of such use and have been convicted in the public opinion (Roger Clemens, Sammy Sosa), essentially making them users, and still others are more the subject of loud whispers of their usage (Mike Piazza, Jeff Bagwell). And none of them, for the second consecutive year, were elected. Some have been on the ballot longer, but last year was the first time for the "big three" of Bonds, Clemens, and Sosa, as well as Piazza and Bagwell, on the ballot – which made last year's vote a true anti-PED referendum. I wrote about that vote last January, and the link to that post is below.

119

This year's vote, as to the drug crowd (whether admitted, convicted, or suspected), was not much different from 2013. None of the players noted above gained admission, and only former Astros' star Craig Biggio (who seems to be collateral damage, linked to his ex-teammate, Bagwell), Piazza, and Bagwell gained over 50% of the vote. Biggio, in fact, fell only two votes short and should gain entry at some point in the future (although maybe not next year, when the ballot will also include first-time shoo-ins Randy Johnson, Pedro Martinez, and John Smoltz (along with steroid-using Gary Sheffield). Piazza earned over 62% of the vote, more than last year, so perhaps the whispers of his usage will be quieted enough to earn the best offensive catcher in baseball history his place in Cooperstown's hallowed hall. Bagwell's 54% may also bode well for him in the future.

The other tainted players did not fare as well as Piazza and Bagwell, gaining the following percentages of the vote: Clemens (35.4%), Bonds (34.7%), McGwire (11%), Sosa (7%), and Palmeiro (4%). Clearly, the referendum against those who have admitted such usage, or who the writers truly believe were users, continues. These five players constitute not only the greatest pitcher and four of the most prolific hitters of the era, but, legitimately, one of the greatest pitchers and three of the greatest hitters (I am excluding McGwire, whom I still consider to be a juiced version of Dave Kingman) ever to step onto the baseball diamond. Clearly, the ethically-high-road taking voters are keeping these players out for doing exactly what the lords of baseball condoned while they were still playing – enhancing their bodies so that they could enhance their statistics – which, inevitably, enhanced attendance and, most importantly, enhanced the coffers of the team owners.

It is not my intention, however, to dispute the votes that keep these players from the Hall. From my perspective, the votes against them are not as much about the drug usage as it is about their conduct since. Bonds claims that he never knew what he was taking, so he never did anything intentionally. Clemens somehow continues to maintain his innocence even in the face of mountains of evidence against him. They have each been the subject of court action for lying to both Congress and the American public. Sosa and Palmeiro both failed to recall using such substances when testifying before Congress, Palmeiro famously wagging his finger against his inquisitors as if to admonish them for even asking him if he was a user – and then, of course, he tested positive for such use thereafter. So perhaps it is their defiance that keeps the doors to the Hall barred.

*****

This time every year, someone raises the call for Pete Rose to gain entry into the Hall – on one hand, it does seem a shame that baseball's all-time hits leader is denied his rightful place; at the same time, however, there are several reasons why he should not be inducted: first, and the most public reason, is that he bet on baseball games, therefore violating one of the most sacred rules of the game. The other reasons are that he voluntarily accepted a lifetime ban from baseball, which seems to bar him from entry, and that he famously denied ever betting on baseball for decades before finally admitting the truth in a tell-all book. Think about it – he lied for years, and then only told the truth in order to make money selling books. It was the ultimate "f#$% you" to baseball, and the rulers of the game are not that forgiving. So Pete's never going to get in – and those others who continue their defiance and denials may, ultimately, continue to join him on the outside.

*****

The disclosure of this year's Hall's vote also coincided with two other news stories, each of which also bears, to a certain extent, on the Hall's unwritten policy of keeping the steroid users out of its roster. The first concerns the continued prosecution of Alex Rodriguez. Rumors abound that the arbitrator's decision as to his suspension may be handed down this weekend. There were rumors that it could have been delivered days ago, but that it was delayed so as not

121

to interfere with the induction announcement or introduction of the newest members of the elite. Based on his numbers, Alex Rodriguez is no different, really, than Bonds or Sosa. He is among the top home-run hitters of all-time, like those two players. He has multiple MVP awards, like Bonds. He is widely suspected of having used PED's, like both, and has been convicted in the court of public opinion. Like Bonds, he also admitted using in the past.

Even as we await the Arbitrator's decision, however, we, as the public, still have not seen a positive drug test regarding the man whose nickname has been altered, by many, to "A-Roid." Perhaps such a test will be revealed when the suspension is upheld, at least in part, and A-Rod's ridiculously large and loud legal team makes good on its promise to seek an injunction in court. He never tested positive in the past, although he did admit using between 2001 and 2003. So when his handlers and supporters point out that a 211-game suspension was extreme since he never tested positive, perhaps there is some truth to that position. Perhaps. Whether or not the suspension is upheld, however, there is little doubt that, unless the Hall doors suddenly swing open for players like Bonds and Clemens, then there will not be a plaque honoring A-Rod five years after his retirement from the game.

There is also a large degree of defiance to Alex Rodriguez, as has clearly been manifested during his appeal of his suspension as well as the various legal machinations which his attorneys have put into place. Much like Bonds and Clemens, this defiance and denial will likely sway voters away from inducting him to the Hall once he becomes eligible. Compare his case, therefore, to that of David Ortiz. As I have previously written, Ortiz has essentially gotten a "get out of jail" card from the writers and fans, despite being named in the past as a PED user, due solely to the fact that he is not a malcontent, and instead is more akin to a large, lovable teddy bear. Ortiz's career numbers are nowhere as great as A-Rod's, but the case can be made that he is one of the best post-season players ever (in direct contrast to Alex's lackluster performances once the calendar turns to October).

With Thomas' induction this year, the Hall may be more likely to welcome players who served predominantly as Designated Hitters (fingers crossed, Edgar Martinez) so the Hall may open its doors to Big Papi Ortiz when he hangs up his bat. Despite the allegations against him, and despite his wrongful denials. He may be elected because he smiles, instead of scowling.

*****

The other story, which has not been as widely-reported, was the death this week of former Philadelphia sports columnist Bill Conlin at the age of 79. Conlin was a long-time writer, his columns gracing newspapers in the City of Brotherly Love for the better part of five decades, and often a guest on ESPN's *The Sports Reporters*. Bill Conlin also gained Hall of Fame status in 2011 as the winner of the J.G. Taylor Spink Award. Months later, however, he resigned his position with the *Philadelphia Daily News* amid allegations of child abuse four decades earlier. He was never prosecuted for the alleged crimes due to the lapse of time, but the allegations, clearly, were the death knell to his career.

The day he resigned his position, the secretary/treasurer of the BBWAA, those who vote on induction into the Hall of Fame and the Spink Award, issued a "member in good standing" statement on Conlin's behalf, which read, in part, that the allegations had no bearing on his winning the Spink Award, "which was in recognition of his notable career as a baseball writer."

*****

The Baseball Hall of Fame, presumably, is populated by the best players, managers, and other contributors who have ever been associated with the game. Its roster, it has often been alleged, includes womanizers, drunks, addicts, and cheaters (Gaylord Perry, famously, threw spitballs throughout his career, a clear violation of baseball's rules), and the off-the-field exploits have generally not barred inclusion. Most importantly, none of those people have been ejected from the Hall after their induction, even if such allegations are made against them.

Conlin is just another example, and the vote of confidence issued on his behalf notes that his career is separate from his private life.

Are the Hall voters simply being overly aggressive in their presumed ethical stance, therefore, in not electing people like Bonds and Clemens? Granted, their use of PED's did have an effect on their playing careers, but Is it wrong to exclude these greats of the game due to their steroid use, even with the knowledge that, had such usage been discovered following induction, their plaques would still be proudly displayed?

But perhaps most damning thing here is the possibility that many of these voters are also not likely beyond reproach. I am not opining as to whether or not Bill Conlin was guilty or not of the allegations against him. Let's assume, for the moment, however, that he was. Up until 2011, he had a vote as to who would be enshrined, and it is conceivable that he failed to vote for McGwire, Bagwell, or Palmeiro, each of whom were on the ballot in 2011. Wouldn't that have been hypocritical? Is the "high road" being taken by these writers, therefore, more sanctimonious than ethical?

Extra Innings: In 2015, the vote totals for those who have been somehow linked to steroid use were as follows: Piazza 69.9%, Bagwell 55.7%, Clemens 37.5%, Bonds 36.8%, Sheffield 11.7%, McGwire 10%, Sosa 6.6%. Absent a dramatic change in the views of the voters, therefore, it appears that Piazza is the only member of the crowd who has a clear chance at gaining entry, and that Bagwell retains an outside shot at joining his teammate, Craig Biggio, who was elected in 2015. Of the new entrants to the ballot in 2016, only Ken Griffey Jr. is a lock for induction. Trevor Hoffman may have a chance, but the Hall is generally not warm to relief pitchers so he likely will not gain entry in his first year of eligibility. The dearth of new entrants should pave the way for Piazza's induction this year, and possibly Bagwell's if the voters can get past the rumors of his alleged PED use.

The real poster children for steroid use, the quartet of Clemens, Bonds, McGwire and Sosa, still have no chance. Their vote totals in 2015 were essentially identical to 2014, and show no signs of increasing.

If I Had a (Hall of Fame) Ballot ...

(Originally posted January 6, 2015)

Today, the voting for the Baseball Hall of Fame class of 2015 will be announced. Voting is done by the Baseball Writers Association of America, and no more than ten votes may be cast on any one ballot. To gain entry, a candidate must be named on at least 75% of all ballots cast. Thus far, there have been no unanimous selections – the highest percentage ever was Tom Seaver's 98.8% - some writers simply believe that there should be no unanimous selections, and will therefore leave obvious candidates off of their ballots.

While I do not have a vote (what's that all about?) if I were to possess such power, the following would be on my ballot for 2015 induction:

The Sure Things

Randy Johnson – 4,875 career strikeouts (second all-time), a member of the 300 victory club, and five Cy Young awards. A no-brainer.

Pedro Martinez – Another member of the 3,000 strikeout club, he won three Cy Young Awards (and also finished twice in the balloting, all within a six-year span of domination rarely matched in baseball history). With a career ERA below 3.00, the only knock against him may be his low win total (219), but his .687 winning percentage (he only had 100 losses) more than makes up for this potential problem. Another no-brainer.

In fact, the only real question with these two is which will receive more votes, and whether either will get a higher percentage than Seaver's record total.

The Almost Definites

Craig Biggio – Jersey guy (Seton Hall graduate) fell only two votes short last year, so he should garner enough support for entry in 2015. His 3,060 career hits, almost 700 doubles, and over 400 stolen bases make a very strong case for induction.

John Smoltz – former Braves pitcher should join 2014 entrants and former teammates Greg Maddux and Tom Glavine in his first year on the ballot. A rare combination of victories (213) and saves (154) (think Dennis Eckersley) and membership in the 3,000 strikeout club create a formidable resume.

Those Who Should Get In, But Likely Won't

Jeff Bagwell – 449 career home runs, a batting average just south of .300, and over 1,500 RBI's and runs scored put him on the cusp of entry, but may not be enough for some writers. It would be great, however, to see both Biggio and Bagwell gain entry in the same year, both of whom would sport Astros' hats on their plaques.

Mike Piazza – the catcher with the best lifetime offensive statistics, Piazza may be denied entry by some due to continued whispers about his alleged steroid usage.

Tim Raines – 2,600 hits, 808 stolen bases (with the highest percentage of stolen base success rate in baseball history), and over 1,500 runs scored should be enough to gain entry, but the prevailing wisdom seems to be that he will again fall short of induction.

Those Who Aren't Getting Support, For Reasons I Can't Understand

Fred McGriff – Granted, he was not the flashiest player ever, but the "Crime Dog" retired with 493 career homers (the same amount as another not-so-flashy first baseman, Lou Gehrig), and 1,550 RBI's to go along with his 441 career doubles and three Silver Slugger awards. It appears that he is essentially being penalized for not succumbing to the temptations of steroid use. Never has he been linked to any such usage, and his numbers are therefore somewhat lower than his contemporaries who did use (McGwire, Palmeiro, etc).

Edgar Martinez – Martinez retired as one of the best Designated Hitters ever, and potentially the best pure hitter north of the late Tony Gwynn. A .312 lifetime batting average, he compiled over 2,200 hits, won the Silver Slugger award five times and made seven All-Star games.

My Sentimental Choice, But I'm Not Even Sure He Should Be In

Mike Mussina – Mussina will get votes because he pitched in the strong AL East during the steroid era (for Baltimore and the Yankees) and retired with a career record of 270-153. Only Andy Pettitte had 100 more victories than losses and is not currently in the Hall. Detractors will note, however, his career 3.68 ERA and the fact that he only won 20 games once (in his final season). He is, seemingly, much like Hall member Don Sutton – never the top pitcher in the league (often not even on his own team) but who amassed good-looking numbers over a long career. Sutton, however, is a member of the 300 victory club. Mussina is not. If he does gain entry, it may even be due more to his glove – he did win seven Gold Glove awards (but remember that Jim Kaat, with his 283 victories and 16 Gold Gloves, is not a member).

The above would be the ten players checked "yes" on my ballot. There are others who have been garnering consideration from the pundits, such as Curt Schilling, Lee Smith, and two of baseball's steroid "poster children" – Barry Bonds and Roger Clemens – but I have no room for them on my already full ballot. Not that I would even consider voting for Bonds or Clemens, mind you, or Mark McGwire or Sammy Sosa, not only because of their steroid usage, but more due to their petulant denials with respect to same.

Of course, reasonable minds may differ. At 2:00 PM today, we will know the decisions of those fortunate enough to actually have a say.

Extra Innings: Not that it was overly difficult to predict, but I was a perfect four-for-four. The 2015 Hall of Fame class consisted of, in alphabetical order, Craig Biggio, Randy Johnson, Pedro Martinez, and John Smoltz. Johnson received 97.3% of the vote, Martinez 91.1%, Smoltz 82.9%, and Biggio 82.7%.

Randy Johnson to Wear D'Backs Hat in HOF ... But Why??

(Originally posted January 17, 2015)

It has been announced that Randy Johnson will be sporting an Arizona Diamondbacks' hat on his Hall of Fame plaque. While some residents of the great Northwest may cry foul, and that Johnson should be wearing a Seattle Mariners' hat, the reality is that Johnson did enjoy some of his best seasons while in Arizona, so it is not totally shocking that he will be immortalized with their cap, It does appear, however, that there are also some other potential reasons for the "Big Unit" to be the first Arizona-topped player in the Hall – as opposed to being the first entrant to don a Mariners hat.

First, it seems proper to examine his careers in each city:

	Years	Wins	Strikeouts	Shutouts	Cy Young	All-Star
Seattle	10	130	2,162	19	1	5
Arizona	8	118	2,077	14	4	5

The statistics are pretty close – but he had more seasons, victories, strikeouts, and shutouts while pitching in Seattle – the city where he first rose to prominence as an ace starting pitcher. On the other hand, he won three more Cy Young Awards while in the heat of the southwest, and also captured his only World Series ring while with the D'Backs (in 2001 over the Yankees). The Cy Young Awards and World Series championship would normally be enough to tip the scales in Arizona's favor, but – as is so often the case – there is more to this scenario than meets the eye …

His new employer

On the same day that he was elected to the Hall of Fame, it was announced that Johnson would be joining the Diamondbacks' front office as a "special Assistant to the President and CEO" – a position which sounds like little more than a ceremonial title. This announcement was eerily reminiscent of 1993, when it was announced on the eve of the Hall of Fame announcement that Reggie Jackson had been hired by one of his former teams, the Yankees, to work in their front office. Shortly thereafter, Jackson announced that he would be wearing a Yankees' hat in the Hall, much to the chagrin of Oakland A's fans. You see, Jackson had begun his career with the A's, and had amassed far better statistics with that team than with the Yankees:

	Years	HRs	RBIs	SBs	MVP	All-Star
A's	10	269	776	145	1	6
Yankees	5	144	461	41	0	5

Also, Jackson did win two World Series titles with the Yankees, but he won three rings with Oakland (in consecutive seasons, from 1972 through 1974, although he did not play in the 1972 series due to injury). And unlike Johnson, the numbers are not even close. There is no legitimate reason why Jackson should be donning the interlocking "NY" on his plaque hat, other than the fact that the Yankees hired him and put him on their payroll – and it is also important to remember that when he left New York for California, it was not on good terms. Had the Yankees not hired him on "Hall of Fame eve", there is little doubt that the letter "A" would be resting atop his head on the plaque.

In fact, following some acrimony as to whether Dave Winfield would go into the Hall as a Padre or Yankee in 2001 (Winfield had a longer tenure and better statistics in New York, but was embroiled in a bitter feud with the team's owner, the late George Steinbrenner), it was announced that the Hall of Fame itself would select which hat a player would wear. In 2010, Andre Dawson expressed disappointment that the Hall determined that he would be wearing an Expos' hat rather than that of the Cubs, despite his preference to don a Chicago cap. Gary Carter wanted to go in as a Met, where he won his only World Series title, but the Hall instead enshrined him with the same hat as Dawson, that of the Expos. The idea of a player being "bought" reached new heights when there were stories that Wade Boggs made a deal with Tampa Bay to wear a Rays' cap on his plaque (he did play there for two whole years) but instead he is properly wearing a Red Sox hat.

So did Johnson have any input into the decision? It appears that the Hall consults with the player but then makes its own decision. Perhaps Johnson's recent hiring by the D'Backs did sway the end result, or maybe it was …

The Hall's Desire to Have More Teams Represented

Johnson will be the first player to have a Diamondbacks' hat on his plaque. This may be a reason for the Hall to select this hat, to broaden the scope of represented teams.

But wait, the Mariners' faithful may cry – how long do we have to wait to have the first Mariner in the Hall of Fame?

Not long, Mariners' faithful. One year, to be exact. Next year, Ken Griffey, Jr. is a sure-fire first-ballot Hall of Fame selection. And Griffey, who spent the overwhelming part of his career and put up staggering statistics while in Seattle, will unquestionably be wearing a Mariners' hat – unlike the D'Backs, who do not have any other "certain" candidates in the pipeline. And if seemingly ageless Ichiro Suzuki ever retires, he will also enter the Hall with his Mariners' cap atop his head. Ditto for Edgar Martinez, who should gain entry if the Hall voters wake up and recognize his contributions to the team, albeit as a designated hitter.

131

Making the Mariners wait one more year and then having both teams represented, therefore, seems to be a good political move by the Hall of Fame directors.

Or maybe the Hall did select the Diamondbacks just because Johnson's career there, while briefer, was more dominating – or based solely on the Cy Young awards. We will never know for sure, but it is interesting to ponder.

Does Pete Rose Really Want This Plaque In the Hall of Fame?

(Originally posted February 12, 2015)

The topic of Pete Rose and whether he should enter Major League Baseball's Hall of Fame has again become a hot topic, in the wake of Rob Manfred's recent ascension to the post of MLB Commissioner. Rose was banned from baseball in 1989 for betting on baseball games while he was the manager of the Cincinnati Reds, voluntarily accepting this lifetime suspension in an agreement with then-Commissioner Bart Giamatti despite his public denials as to whether or not he had ever gambled on games involving his team. For years now, however, he has lobbied for reinstatement to the game and to be enshrined in the sport's most hallowed halls ... after finally admitting, in an autobiography, that he had, in fact, bet on games involving his team.

This writer's opinion is that Rose should not be reinstated. The prohibition against gambling on games was, is, and will continue to be baseball's most serious infraction. One need only to look back to the 1919 World Series, the "Black Sox" scandal, and the lifetime suspensions that resulted from that series – including Joe Jackson – as a precedent for Rose's ban. And it is critical to remember that he voluntarily accepted a lifetime ban; only thereafter did he change his mind. Lastly, his petulance – his complete denials of the truth for decades, also should keep him on the outside looking in.

Some now say that he should be let into the Hall, but that his plaque should reference the suspension and gambling. A similar "marking" on Hall of Fame plaques has also been urged for those players caught up in the steroids and PED scandal, should they be voted into the Hall, but in reality, wouldn't such plaques be a cautionary tale of "be careful what you wish for?" relative to these players?

Think about it. Pete Rose wants to be in the Hall of Fame – but does he really want his plaque to read as follows:

The man known as "Charlie Hustle" retired as baseball's all-time hit leader, with 4,256 career hits. A career .303 hitter, Rose won the 1973 Most Valuable Player award and amassed over 200 hits in nine seasons. A 17-time All-Star, he was the National League's Rookie of the Year in 1963. Rose was banned from baseball in 1989 due to gambling on baseball, including games involving the Cincinnati Reds, the team that he was managing at the time. Rose eventually admitted to gambling on such games in his autobiography, and then shamelessly spent the next decade lobbying for reinstatement to the game.

Probably not. And what of the steroid players like Barry Bonds and Roger Clemens? Do they really want for their plaques to reference the negative side of their careers?

Baseball's all-time home run leader with 762 round-trippers, Bonds also holds the single-season record for home runs with 73, set in 2001. A 14-time All-Star, he won the National League Most Valuable Player Award a record seven times, including four consecutive seasons from 2001-2004. Retired with 2,935 hits, and was unable to reach the milestone 3,000 hit club when no team wanted to sign him after a 2007 campaign in which he slugged 28 home runs in only 126 games, due to the fact that he was accused of using anabolic steroids supplied by BALCO. Bonds admitted taking the steroids, but claimed that he did not know what he was taking. He also claimed a lack of knowledge as to why his body grew so much during the time that he was taking substances from BALCO, including his head, which swelled to a size much larger than his earlier playing days. He was later brought up on charges of committing perjury to Congress.

Clemens, known as "The Rocket", won 354 games over a 23-year career with four teams. He struck out 4,672 batters during his career, during which he was named to eleven All-Star teams and seven Cy Young Awards and the 1986 Most Valuable Player Award in the American League. Clemens won 192 games with the Boston Red Sox, and was then labeled as being through by the Boston General Manager. He resurrected his career in Toronto in 1997, capturing consecutive Cy Young Awards for the Blue Jays in 1997 and 1998 before signing with the Yankees. It was in Toronto, allegedly, that his steroid usage began, which many feel accounts for his career renaissance at that time. Clemens has steadfastly denied taking any steroids, despite testimony from others, including friend and major leaguer Andy Pettitte, that he was a

steroid user. Clemens also faced perjury charges arising out of his denials as to such PED use.

And what of the players who have been accused, but against whom no actual proof has been presented – like Mike Piazza, who will likely be enshrined next year? Do they also require such references on their plaques?

Baseball's all-time leading slugger at catcher, Piazza amassed 427 home runs and 1,335 RBI's over a 16-year career spent primarily with the Dodgers and Mets. A 12-time All-Star, he won the National League Rookie of the Year award in 1993 and captured ten Silver Slugger awards and finished in the Top 10 of MVP voting seven times. Due to the surprising power exhibited by a man who selected in round 62 of the draft by the Dodgers in 1988, as well as the fact that he allegedly had "bacne", he has been accused of using performance enhancing substances. No evidence of such use, however, has ever been located.

Will the Hall also be forced to change some of the existing plaques, retroactively, in order to comply with its new-found "open door" enshrinement? Ferguson Jenkins, who was elected to the Hall in 1991, had been arrested in Toronto for possession of cocaine, hashish, and marijuana – while he was still an active player. Does a codicil need to be added to Jenkins' plaque so that his drug usage is reflected? And what of Mickey Mantle? Does his plaque need to be amended to reflect his alcoholism? Ty Cobb's to show that he was a racist? The list goes on and on.

*****

Simply put, the idea of noting these transgressions on a player's Hall of Fame plaque is ludicrous. If I were Rose, Bonds, or Clemens, I would have to think long and hard about whether I would even want to be enshrined under such circumstances – because sometimes absence is better than a negative presence.

Be careful what you wish for, Pete – and remember, if Rob Manfred does the right thing, it should not even be an issue, because you should not be allowed into the Hall of Fame. Not even for the gambling, but for lying for so long. Let your petulance and resulting banishment serve as a message for all who come after you.

Extra Innings: **Commissioner Manfred has stated that he will rule on Rose's reinstatement petition before the end of December 2015. If it were up to me, as noted above, he would not be reinstated. According to one website, MyTopSportsBooks.com, the odds on Rose gaining reinstatement are 8 to 1. Better odds are that he's betting against himself, so that no matter how the Commissioner rules, Rose still wins ... one way or the other. That's the gambler's mentality.**

CHAPTER 5 – IN MEMORIAM

Remembering Thurman Munson - A Salute to the Captain

(Originally posted August 2, 2013)

34 years ago today, August 2, 1979, Yankee catcher and Captain Thurman Munson died in a plane crash in Canton, Ohio. Munson, an amateur pilot, died while practicing takeoffs and landings during a mid-season off-day. His tragic death stunned the baseball world, and ripped the heart and soul of the team from the Yankees' roster, a loss from which it took years to recover.

Munson first broke into the major leagues with the Yankees in 1969, and in 1970, his first full season, he captured the American League's Rookie of the Year award. The first of seven All-Star game appearances followed in 1971, and from 1975 through 1977, he drove in 100 or more runs each season. From 1973 through 1975, he won three consecutive "Golden Glove" awards, as the league's best defensive catcher.

Then, in 1976, he was named the American League's Most Valuable Player following a season in which he amassed 17 Home Runs, 105 Runs Batted In, 14 Stolen Bases, and a .302 batting average. He is one of only three catchers in history to claim both the Rookie of the Year and MVP Awards, along with Hall of Famer Johnny Bench and current Giants' backstop Buster Posey. That was also the year that the Yankees returned to the World Series for the first time in over a decade, and Munson was the best player on a Yankee team that was swept by the Reds in the Fall Classic. The team returned to October glory the next two years, however, winning the World Series in both 1977 and 1978 over the Dodgers. In those three World Series appearances, Munson totaled 12 RBI to go with his stellar .373 batting average, including an amazing .529 average in the 1976 loss to Cincinnati.

Munson amassed those totals while toiling in the large shadows cast by two of his contemporaries, a pair of Hall of Fame catchers widely regarded among the best who have ever played the position – Boston's Carlton Fisk and Cincinnati's Johnny Bench. The often unfavorable comparisons to Fisk reportedly irked Munson, who believed that he was a better player than the Red Sox catcher and, according to reports, was jealous of the attention and praise lavished upon Fisk's play – especially after Fisk's iconic home run captured Game 6 of the 1975 World Series for the Red Sox.

What set Munson apart from most other players was his intensity – there are videos of him basically crawling across the plate to get back into his catcher's position. He played in 140 games or more from 1972 through 1978, allowing little to preclude him from taking his stance behind the batter. This is in sharp contrast to the prima donnas, "Sportscenter" showoffs, and "me-first" players who populate the game today – Munson probably never even heard of an "oblique" muscle, the injury *du jour* that keeps so many players sidelined, and there is no doubt that he would not have allowed such a muscle strain to keep him out of the lineup.

I still remember how I heard about Munson's death. Like people who can recall where they were when they heard about President Kennedy being assassinated, about John Lennon being shot, and other tragedies, many Yankee fans can pinpoint their being told of Munson's crash. This was before 24-hour sports channels. It was before the internet, before cell phones, and before email or texting. I was upstairs in my room when the phone rang – it was a friend of my brother's and fellow Yankees' calling to tell me. It was 1979. I was 13 years old, yet I remember it like it was yesterday.

On a team full of superstars, Munson was the Yankee Captain. Despite Reggie Jackson's proclamation upon joining the Yankees in 1977 that he would be the "straw" that "stirred the drink," clearly the Yankees were Munson's team. He was their heart and soul. He was the first Captain named by the Yankees since the great Lou Gehrig, another player whose career was cut short by tragedy. He played with grit and determination, as noted above, which is not exhibited by more than a handful of players today – Dustin Pedroia of the Red Sox leaps to mind as an example. Munson's gruff exterior may have turned some away, but his clubhouse leadership, even in a locker room full of stars, was never disputed.

A couple of days later, the team flew to Ohio for the funeral, and then back for a game that evening – a game that they insisted on playing. It was a greatly emotional day, of course, and became a day of legend when Bobby Murcer, who had delivered the eulogy for his good friend only hours earlier, drove in all five of the Yankees' runs in a dramatic come-from-behind victory over Baltimore. Tears filled Murcer's eyes following his game-winning hit. The same was true for millions watching the game on television that evening.

His death also was a death knell for Yankee hopes of postseason success in 1979, and led to a protracted post-season dry spell – the Yankees did win the Eastern Division in 1980 and 1981, and returned to the World Series in 1981, but did not again win the championship until 1996, a span of 18 years between World Series titles, the longest in Yankees' history.

Munson's legacy with the Yankees has been cemented in various forms – his number 15 has been retired by the team (and many fans still wear their number "15" jerseys to Yankees' games), and he has been honored with a plaque in Yankee Stadium's Monument Park. Most notably, his locker was retired after his death, never to be used again. When the Yankees moved to their new stadium several years ago, his locker was removed and placed into the stadium's Yankees Museum, where it remains today.

So on this day, August 2, 2013, we again remember Thurman Munson, Yankee Captain. We recall his contributions to the Yankees on and off the field, and wonder what could have been. We still miss you, Captain.

BLOGGIN' BASEBALL II (FROM THE BLEACHERS) - ANDREW WOLFENSON

One more thing – the well-publicized feud between Munson and Reggie Jackson led to a great deal of sniping between them. Jackson, famously, said that he would be the star of the team and, as noted above, the "straw that stirred the drink." He also claimed that the other players were jealous of his stardom. In response, Munson told Jackson that he had no reason to be jealous – as detailed in his autobiography, posted in 1978, Munson wrote:

"I have things in life which Reggie can only hope to have – a stable family life with a wife and three great children; a secure private business life which has kept my head in the real world and provided lifetime security for my family; genuine friends, maintained from my years in Canton... I think when I confronted him with the reality of life – that baseball may be a great ego trip, but there's a lot more in this world than baseball – he found himself unable to deal with it."

Intensity, tremendous baseball ability, and perfect perspective on the game and its relative importance to life. No wonder he was, and always will be, the Captain.

The Silencing of Two Iconic New York Voices

(Originally posted August 25, 2013)

Earlier this week, the New York area lost one of its television icons, Bill Mazer. In a time before cable television, in a time before 24-hour news and sports networks, the residents of the New York area had several methods by which to obtain their sports information. We had the network sports guys, like Marv Albert and Warner Wolf. On Saturdays, we had "This Week in Baseball" with the great Mel Allen.

And on Channel 5, we had the great Bill Mazer. Nicknamed "The Amazin'," Mazer hosted "Sports Extra" on Sunday nights following the nightly newscast – it was, for some, the most comprehensive half-hour of sports reporting that we could watch. And we did. All of us watched Mazer report the sports and, perhaps more impressively, answer trivia question after trivia question on a live call-in segment. It was called "Stump the Amazin'," and Mazer rarely, if ever, did not know the answer to the question posed, whether it be about baseball, football, or even horse racing. He was calm, cool, and collected.

Actually, he was completely unflappable, even on one occasion when a caller said, "I want to f$%^ your wife, you Jew bastard." Mazer simply hung up the call, remarked that there were pitfalls in a live broadcast, and moved onto the next caller. He was the epitome of class and possessed an encyclopedia of sports in his mind. Compare his breadth of knowledge to the complete lack of fundamental knowledge possessed by one of the people who passes as a "sports host" today – several years ago, the following exchange took place between Chris "Mad Dog" Russo, then at WFAN, and former baseball star Jim Kaat:

Russo: *"So Jim, what was it like being elected to the Hall of Fame?"*

Kaat: *"Uh, Chris, I'm not in the Hall of Fame."*

Russo: "You're not? That's a shame."

Bill Mazer died this week at the age of 92. His class, his professionalism, and his knowledge of sports was, and continues to be, unmatched. All wanna-be sportscasters should be forced to watch tapes of his "Sports Extra" shows to see how their craft should be practiced.

On behalf of a generation of NY sports fans, Bill, thank you for enriching our childhood and our love of sports. You will be missed.

*****

If Bill Mazer represented the sports reporting of my formative years, it is not a stretch to say that WNEW-FM was the radio station of my youth. New York's premier rock station at the time, WNEW boasted radio voices that were widely recognized as the best in the business. Scott Muni was thought by many to be the dean of radio voices, but a strong argument could be advanced that Dave Herman was not far behind.

Today's *Newark Star-Ledger* is reporting that Herman, now 77 years old, was arrested at the St. Croix airport. According to the article, he is being charged with "trying to transport a 7-year old Bergen County girl to the U.S. Virgin Islands to sexually abuse her there."

The article continues as follows: "[t]hough no girl existed – she was the creation of an undercover officer from the Bergen County Prosecutor's Office who met Herman as he allegedly trolled the internet – Herman faces a mandatory minimum of 10 years in prison and a maximum penalty of life, if convicted. He is charged with attempting to transport a minor in interstate commerce with the intent that the minor engage in sexual activity."

According to authorities, Herman said that "I find girls that age incredibly sexy, soft, and their innocence is also a huge turn on for me."

There's really little that can be said about these allegations, other than that they are shocking, perverse, and present a side of the former radio icon that was, up until now, completely unknown to his legion of fans. And completely disappointing.

*****

So this week, the New York area has had two of its iconic 1970's era voices silenced. The late, great Bill Mazer has been taken from us at the ripe old age of 92, leaving behind a legacy of class, dignity, and unparalleled professionalism. Former voice of WNEW Dave Herman sits behind bars, accused of attempting to lure a 7-year old girl to the Virgin Islands in order to force her to participate in sexual acts with him. His previous record of class and professionalism is forever tarnished. And that, to me, is even sadder than Mazer's death.

Jimmy V and Lou Gehrig - Two Great and Courageous Speeches

(Originally posted July 16, 2014)

"Today I consider myself the luckiest man on the face of the earth."

- *Lou Gehrig*

"Don't give up. Don't ever give up."

- *Jim Valvano*

Earlier this month marked 75 years since former Yankees' first baseman Lou Gehrig, dying of the disease which would eventually bear his name, told a hushed Yankee Stadium crowd that he had "an awful lot to live for." 21 years ago, former North Carolina State basketball coach Jim Valvano, dying of cancer, told a rapt ESPY awards crowd that he was going to try to live each of his remaining days to the fullest.

Gehrig died two years after his speech. Valvano passed away a scant month after his. These two courageous men, each of whom stepped to a microphone and delivered positive words despite their dire fates, will be forever linked as the deliverers of two of the most inspirational speeches in sports history, if not history in general.

The ESPY awards air tonight on ESPN, and the network's radio station has devoted much of its programming today to raising money for the "Jimmy V Fund for Cancer Research", the fund established by ESPN when Valvano was sick and which was announced by Valvano during his stirring speech two decades ago. The station played the eight-minute speech in its entirety, and Jimmy V's stirring words and call to action for increased cancer research resonate as powerfully today as they did then, much like Gehrig's speech reverberated well beyond the Bronx back in 1939.

147

"Fans, for the past two weeks you have been reading about the bad break I got. Yet today I consider myself the luckiest man on the face of this earth. I have been in ballparks for seventeen years and have never received anything but kindness and encouragement from you fans."

Gehrig, baseball's "Iron Man," had played in 2,130 consecutive games prior to removing himself from the Yankees' lineup as his disease progressed and his health and abilities deteriorated. He was diagnosed with Amyotrophic Lateral Sclerosis (now commonly known as "Lou Gehrig's Disease") and the diagnosis was essentially a death sentence, although he sought to keep the severity of the disease a secret from the public and those around him. The courage which he exhibited in speaking before the crowd that day, therefore, amplified his words more than the Stadium's PA system could ever accomplish. This is especially true in light of the positive vibe that ran through his speech:

"When the New York Giants, a team you would give your right arm to beat, and vice versa, sends you a gift - that's something. When everybody down to the groundskeepers and those boys in white coats remember you with trophies - that's something. When you have a wonderful mother-in-law who takes sides with you in squabbles with her own daughter - that's something. When you have a father and a mother who work all their lives so you can have an education and build your body - it's a blessing. When you have a wife who has been a tower of strength and shown more courage than you dreamed existed - that's the finest I know."

Gehrig, as noted above, lived for another two years before succumbing to ALS. Letters written by him to his doctors and wife, included in a recent biography, seem to suggest that he did not even know the severity of his condition. Valvano, however, gave his speech armed with the knowledge that his days were limited. Invited to the ESPY awards to receive the initial Arthur Ashe award for courage, it was doubtful that he could even attend the ceremony, much less give

148

any form of acceptance speech. According to those who flew to New York with him, he was sick the entire flight and merely getting to the Paramount Theater for the ceremony was a feat in and of itself. When the appointed hour arrived, however, he was helped up the steps to the podium and, once he was standing behind the microphone, he more than rallied to the occasion.

"Time is very precious to me. I don't know how much I have left and I have some things that I would like to say. Hopefully, at the end, I will have said something that will be important to other people too."

And did he ever, in a speech marked by words both poignant and comedic. His sharp wit was showcased when the show's producers tried to cut his speech short, in the middle of his discussion of his family ...

"I talked about my family, my family's so important. People think I have courage. The courage in my family are my wife Pam, my three daughters, here, Nicole, Jamie, LeeAnn, my mom, who's right here too. That screen is flashing up there thirty seconds like I care about that screen right now, huh? I got tumors all over my body. I'm worried about some guy in the back going thirty seconds? You got a lot, hey va fa napoli, buddy. You got a lot."

He went on to discuss the need for additional cancer research, the establishment of the Jimmy V fund, and, of course, to tell more stories. He concluded the speech with words that showed his true spirit – the spirit of a fighter:

"I got one last thing and I said it before, and I want to say it again. Cancer can take away all my physical abilities. It cannot touch my mind, it cannot touch my heart and it cannot touch my soul. And those three things are going to carry on forever."

And they do, in the form of the Foundation which bears his name. Just like Lou Gehrig's name lives on not just for his accomplishments on the baseball diamond, but as the commonly-known name for a previously-unknown disease, so that research monies are easier to come by. Valvano asked for donations for cancer research not just for his sake, but for the sake of others, that someone might be saved in the future through his efforts. That result is unquestioned. The Foundation has raised millions over the past two decades, and no doubt has saved thousands of lives.

Lou Gehrig's monument at Yankee Stadium

The closing words of Gehrig's speech were simple, befitting the quiet way in which the "Iron Horse," one of the greatest players ever, played the game - *"So I close in saying that I may have had a tough break, but I have an awful lot to live for."*

On the other end of the spectrum, Valvano, the boisterous New Yorker who never met a microphone that he did not like, provided a road map for others to lead their lives: *"To me, there are three things we all should do every day. We should do this every day of our lives. Number one is laugh. You should laugh every day. Number two is think. You should spend some time in thought. Number three is, you should have your emotions moved to tears, could be happiness or joy. But think about it. If you laugh, you think, and you cry, that's a full day. That's a heck of a day. You do that seven days a week, you're going to have something special."*

I think of these words every day, and try to accomplish all three so that I have what Jimmy V considered to be a "full day." More often than not, I am successful. Truth be told, I satisfied all three just writing this post. Hopefully you have done all three while reading it.

Extra Innings: That evening's ESPY broadcast included a speech from a man whose message and classy defiance rivaled those of Gehrig and Valvano. SportsCenter host Stuart Scott, in the midst of an on-going battle with cancer, was presented with the Jimmy V Award for Perseverance. Like Valvano, he essentially went from sick bed to the ceremony, and in a clear, resonant voice which masked the cancer ravaging his body, gave an inspirational speech that left the assembled crowd in tears. "When you die," Scott said, "it does not mean that you lose to cancer. You beat cancer by how you live, why you live, and the manner in which you live."

Stuart Scott passed away on January 4, 2015. His book, "Every Day I Fight," was published shortly after his death and is a must-read for any sports fan … or father.

BLOGGIN' BASEBALL II (FROM THE BLEACHERS) - ANDREW WOLFENSON

Ernie Banks, "Mr. Cub", Dies at 83

(Originally posted January 24, 2015)

Ernie Banks, the man affectionately known as "Mr. Cub", died last night at the age of 83. A 1977 inductee into the baseball Hall of Fame and a 2013 recipient of the Presidential Medal of Freedom, Banks' death closes yet another chapter of major league baseball's glorious past, an era which it appears, sadly, will never be experienced by today's youth.

It is simple to recite Banks' statistics – 19 seasons, all with the Cubs (he was also the first African-American player to don the Cubs' uniform). 512 career home runs, 1,636 career runs batted in, 2,583 hits. He was selected for eleven All-Star game appearances, and won back-to-back Most Valuable Player Awards in 1958 and 1959.

And he attained all of this glory while playing for a sub-par team – in one way, Ernie Banks was the ultimate measure of baseball futility – he played in 2,528 career games with the Cubs – the most ever by a player who never played in the post-season (playoffs or World Series).

But to refer to Banks as a failure would be completely erroneous – rather, his career can only be viewed as triumphant, because no matter how bad his Cubs' teams were, he played with unbridled and unparalleled passion – coining the phrase "let's play two" because he always wanted to play another game. His love for the game, his joy at being on the diamond, transcended the losing nature of his teams and further endeared him to Chicago's long-suffering fans.

For the past 60 years he has been, literally, the embodiment of his nickname. He has been the face of the Cubs' franchise, and a positive ambassador of both the team and city. He was a throwback to a simpler time in sports, one unassailed by 24-hour news networks and TMZ-like investigations. He remained the smiling face of an embattled franchise, one which has not won a World Series in what seems like forever, and a team which seems poised to make a possible playoff run this season – but a season which will now not be shared by its all-time greatest player.

Major league baseball believes itself to be at a crossroads – simply put, its fan base is getting older. The league has reportedly done studies into how to increase its popularity amongst this country's youth, how to get the youngsters as interested in baseball as they are in football and basketball. One easy way to do so, trite though it may seem, is through hero worship. Kids want to be their favorite basketball players – LeBron James, Kevin Durant, etc – the guys they see on nightly highlight films, in commercials, the ones with larger-than-life personalities. Baseball needs guys like LeBron. It doesn't have any.

Derek Jeter retired last year. He retired as the undisputed "face of baseball" and was clearly the face of the Yankees' franchise. He left behind a sport devoid of a clear successor, a sport where individuality is stifled and players are taught to hide underneath their cap rather than express themselves on the field – and when players like Yasiel Puig bring enthusiasm to the field like he had done while playing in Cuba, he is smacked down as being overly demonstrative. Baseball players do not have nationwide endorsement deals. There are no players who are truly Banks or Jeter-like, especially due to the lack of enthusiasm, the lack of high-profile endorsements, and continuing player movements in free agency. Names of young players like Mike Trout of the Angels and Bryce Harper of the Nationals are the first names that leap to mind, but Harper got into some hot water for missing a fanfest last year – an event that Banks, who continued to attend Cub-fan-related events for years after his retirement, would never have skipped. Then there is Pablo Sandoval, the former darling of the San Francisco bay area, who bolted to the Red Sox this off-season for an additional $5 million in salary. Loyalty to a team and its fan base? Not anymore.

Paul Sullivan of the Chicago Tribune wrote that Banks "made the idea of playing a baseball game under the sun at the corner of Clark and Addison streets sound like a day in paradise, win or lose". We simply do not see such enthusiasm expressed on the field today – partially because it is not permitted, and partially, one can argue, because the "business" has overtaken the "game".

Perhaps nobody expressed the loss of Banks better than Cubs Chairman Tom Ricketts, who released the following statement on the team's behalf:

"Words cannot express how important Ernie Banks will always be to the Chicago Cubs, the city of Chicago and Major League Baseball. He was one of the greatest players of all time. He was a pioneer in the major leagues. And more importantly, he was the warmest and most sincere person I've ever known. Approachable, ever optimistic and kind-hearted, Ernie Banks is and always will be Mr. Cub. My family and I grieve the loss of such a great and good-hearted man, but we look forward to celebrating Ernie's life in the days ahead."

"Let's play two."

The shame is that Ernie Banks could only "live one" – but what a life it was. He will be missed – as Tom Ricketts said – by the Cubs, the City of Chicago, and all of Major League Baseball. And to a larger extent, by anyone who follows baseball or any other sport. The world needs more people like Ernie Banks. The sports world needs more positive role models like Ernie Banks.

R.I.P., Mr. Cub.

Chicago Loses Another Baseball Legend - RIP, Minnie Minoso

(Originally posted March 1, 2015)

The city of Chicago, and the world of Major League Baseball, lost their second ambassador over the past five weeks when White Sox legend Minnie Minoso died yesterday at the age of 90. Minoso is best known to this writer's generation as one of the two players to appear in games over five different decades – to the prior generation, however, he was widely regarded as the first black Latino superstar, and merited induction into the Baseball Hall of Fame with former Cubs' great Ernie Banks, who died in late January.

Minoso's career, to those of us raised in the 70's, was more of a curiosity than one of a possible Hall of Famer. He did appear in games over five decades, but two of the appearances which qualified him as such were publicity stunts at best – a three-game stint in 1976 (as if the White Sox uniforms that season, which featured shorts, were not enough to gain publicity) which yielded one hit in eight at-bats, and two appearances in 1980 in which he was hitless in two at-bats. The stunts which yielded his best-known "accomplishment", however, served to mask a career which – while perhaps not Hall of Fame worthy – was certainly worthy of great respect.

Minoso played on a full-time basis between 1951 and 1963, spending the majority of his career with the White Sox. During that time, he led the American League in hits (1960), doubles (1957), triples (three times) and was a three-time stolen base champion (in his first three full seasons, from 1951-1953). He finished second in the voting for Rookie of the Year in 1951, won three Gold Glove awards, appeared in seven All-Star Games, and, interestingly, finished fourth in Most Valuable Player voting a seemingly appropriate four times. He retired with 1,963 hits and a career batting average of .298 to go with his 186 home runs, 1,023 runs batted in, and 205 career stolen bases. He was also hit by 192 pitches during his career, leading the league in that dubious category on ten occasions.

According to www.minoso.com, billed as the "Minnie Minoso official site", he was the ninth black player in the major leagues, the first to play for the White Sox, and was also the first publicly acknowledged Cuban ballplayer in the majors. Elected into the Chicago Sports Hall of Fame in 1984, he was also enshrined in the World Baseball Hall of Fame in 1990.

Known as the "Cuban Comet," his number 9 was retired by the White Sox in 1983. While he never gained induction to Cooperstown, his effect on the Windy City and its fans rivaled that of the recently-deceased man known as "Mr. Cub" – Cubs Chairman echoed as such in his statement released after Minoso's death, indicating that the Cubs' organization was "deeply saddened by the passing of Minnie Minoso. Having recently lost one of our all-time greats, Ernie Banks, we share the heartache with the White Sox organization and fans everywhere who were blessed to enjoy the talent, heart and passion of Mr. White Sox."

For the second time this year, the city of Chicago has lost one of its legends. And much like the loss of Ernie Banks in late January, the loss of Minnie Minoso leaves a void in the hearts of baseball fans across this country ... and beyond.

CHAPTER 6 – BASEBALL (GENERAL)

It's A Wonderful Life For This Mr. (Homer) Bailey

(Originally posted July 3, 2013)

Last night, Homer Bailey of the Cincinnati Reds completely stifled the bats of the opposing San Francisco Giants, allowing no hits and only one walk en route to a 3-0 victory. In doing so, Bailey cemented his place in baseball history and joined the elite club of pitchers who have hurled multiple no-hitters in their careers. He also joined his idol, Hall of Famer Nolan Ryan, in a fascinating examination of historical significance.

Bailey was born on May 3, 1986 in La Grange, Texas, and grew up idolizing Ryan, the larger-than-life Texan who still holds the major league records for most strikeouts in a career and for most career no-hitters (seven). He proudly wears number 34 across the back of his Reds' jersey in honor of Ryan, who wore that number while pitching for the Texas Rangers. The similarities between the two men, however, run far beyond their uniform numbers and home state.

Bailey's first no-hitter was ten months ago, on September 28, 2012 against Pittsburgh. No other man has thrown a no-no since then, meaning that Bailey is the latest pitcher, and only the seventh in major-league history, to possess the majors' last two consecutive no-hitters. The last player to accomplish this feat before him? Nolan Ryan, of course. Ryan did so in 1974 and 1975 while pitching for the Angels (he wore number 30 at the time, somewhat detracting from the "history repeats itself" theme, but let's put that aside for now). With those two gems, Ryan was also the last pitcher to throw the last no-hitter of one season and the first of the next season – in fact, only three pitchers have ever accomplished this feat –Warren Spahn in 1960 and 1961, Ryan, and now Bailey. Note that Addie Joss pitched the last no-hitter in 1908 and the first in 1910, and there were none in

1909 so he technically can also be added to this list. It is also important to note that Spahn, Ryan, and Joss are all members of Baseball's Hall of Fame.

A little more historical perspective on Bailey's dual no-hitters: in the long and storied history of the Cincinnati Reds, one of baseball's charter organizations, only three men have thrown two no-hitters – Bailey, Johnny Vander Meer and Jim Maloney. Vander Meer, of course, famously holds a special place in the annals of baseball as he was the only pitcher ever to throw no-hitters in consecutive starts. Bailey's, as noted above, were thrown ten months apart – so let's refer to them as "Irish Twin" no-hitters.

One can also compare Bailey's feat to other teams – he has now thrown one more no-hitter than the entire New York Mets team has thrown since it began play in 1962, for example. Also, review of the list of no-hitters reveals that, since the day that Bailey was born 27 years ago (May 3, 1986), a total of 67 such gems have been tossed. Some (six in total) have been group efforts, meaning that more than one pitcher was involved, and the list does include several other pitchers who seemingly were lucky for one evening as the remainder of their careers were anything but stellar, such as Joe Cowley (Chicago), Juan Nieves (Milwaukee), Tom Browning (Cincinnati), Tommy Greene (Philadelphia), Chris Bosio (Seattle), Scott Erickson (Minnesota), Jose Jimenez (St. Louis), Eric Milton (Minnesota), Bud Smith (St. Louis), Dallas Braden (Oakland), and Philip Humber (Chicago).

Some may argue that there have been many such no-hitters recently, which somehow can detract from the majesty of Bailey's feat. There were seven no-hitters thrown in 2012, and 17 have been hurled since the beginning of the 2010 season. Bailey, with two such games, however, has now thrown more no-hitters than a dozen teams have thrown *since he was born*. Even using his major league debut as a marker, June 8, 2007, he is one of only three pitchers to throw two no-hitters during that time span, a select group which includes Bailey, Justin Verlander (his first was only four days after Bailey's debut), and Roy Halladay. Two other pitchers, Mark Buehrle and Kevin Millwood, each pitched one no-no

162

before Bailey entered the league and one thereafter. It is also interesting to note that of Ryan's seven career no-hitters, exactly two were thrown after Bailey's birth, although they were hurled at a time when the then three and four-year-old Bailey was likely too young to have been watching the games and dreaming of replicating his idol's efforts.

It should also be noted that while the San Francisco Giants have seemingly been willing participants on the wrong end of no-hitters for some time (last night was the fifth time that they have been no-hit since Bailey was born), the no-hitter thrown by Bailey last September was the first time that the Pittsburgh Pirates had been the victims of such pitching excellence since they were shut down by Hall of Famer Bob Gibson in 1971, a span of over 40 years.

Any way you look at it, Bailey's feat is nothing short of remarkable. Being mentioned in the same breath as elite pitchers like Ryan, Spahn, Gibson, Verlander, and Vander Meer is, in and of itself, something to be proud of. Being the seventh player in the history of baseball to own the game's last two no-hitters, and only the third member of one of baseball's founding teams to throw two such masterpieces, all add up to an accomplishment worth celebrating.

As was famously said in the classic movie about another man with the last name Bailey - *It's a Wonderful Life* - every time a bell rings, "an angel gets its wings." Here, when the final bell sounded on Homer Bailey's no-hitters of September 28, 2012 and July 2, 2013, he certainly earned praise and accolades for his own wing, the right arm that so baffled the hitters of the Pittsburgh and San Francisco teams.

Extra Innings: An even more impressive sequence was turned in by Washington's Max Scherzer in 2015. On June 14, 2015, he gave up only one hit and one walk to the Brewers, recording 16 strikeouts en route to a 4-0 victory. Six days later, he threw a no-hitter against the Pirates, recording ten strikeouts. In that game, he came within one strike of a perfect game – with two outs in the ninth inning, and two strikes on Jose Tabata, he threw a pitch that hit Tabata – and then ended the game on the next pitch when he induced

Josh Harrison to fly out. Scherzer then threw another gem on October 3 – this time against the Mets. In that game he gave up no hits, no walks, and struck out 17 batters. The only baserunner that day reached on an error. Many consider this game to be one of the greatest pitching performances of all time.

Scherzer is the only pitcher to throw two games in the same season in which he gave up no hits or walks – and except for a hit batsman and throwing error, he would be able to truly boast that he hurled two perfect games in 2015.

Climbing Aboard the Pirates' Ship - I mean, Bandwagon

(Originally posted October 7, 2013)

The Pittsburgh Pirates are one game away from the National League Championship Series, and I could not be happier for them. The Pirates, one of baseball's oldest and most storied franchises, have endured a dry spell of semi-epic proportions, over two decades without a playoff appearance before this season. In fact, they had two decades of consecutive losing seasons, and their rabid fan base was about to enter the stratosphere of ineptitude heretofore occupied solely by forlorn Chicago Cubs fans.

But all of that is a mere memory now, as these young Bucs not only reached the playoffs, but swashbuckled their way past division rivals Cincinnati in the Wild Card game and are now poised to knock their other division rivals, the Cardinals, out of the playoffs with a win at frenzied PNC Park tonight. The stadium will no doubt be packed to the rafters with fans tonight, and thousands more will gather outside of its gates, and along the bridges spanning the adjacent rivers, to witness the latest piece in the Pirates' historic puzzle.

PNC Park, as I have said numerous times in the past, is my favorite baseball stadium – even more so than the new Yankee Stadium. Its retro-look, combined with its homage to both team and baseball history, combine to create a perfect place in which to watch a game. The open outfield, which reveals the skyline and the Roberto Clemente Bridge, is sheer majesty. Based on the stadium alone, the team is worth rooting for. Below are some pictures taken on a tour of the park several years ago.

A picture of me in the Pirates' dugout in 2008. Foreshadowing for my jumping on the band-ship, perhaps

Statue of Roberto Clemente outside of PNC Park, at the base of the Roberto Clemente Bridge

The Pittsburgh skyline as seen through the outfield - that's the Clemente Bridge to the left.

The view from the press box - I mean, seriously? Can it get any better than this? It is breathtaking.

The last time that the Pirates captured baseball's ultimate prize was 1979, the "We are Family" Pirates, led by Captain Willie Stargell. They have captured five such World Series titles, meaning that if they are to win this year's championship they will tie the football Steelers with what their fans affectionately term the "six pack" of rings. The team has boasted numerous all-time greats,

167

including Rogers Hornsby, Paul and Lloyd Waner, Ralph Kiner, Clemente, and Stargell. The team also lays claim to one of the greatest moments in baseball history, Bill Mazeroski's home run which captured the 1960 World Series over the Yankees.

It is the Pirates' time to raise a World Championship banner alongside the Jolly Roger again. Everyone loves an underdog, right? And what better underdog can there be than a team which has its first winning record in 20 years, a team which has AJ Burnett in its starting rotation?

So avast, all fans of teams that did not make the playoffs, the Buc Boat is boarding. Your permission to board is granted, and to join all of us new Pirates' fans as the team steers its course through the postseason. The likely next destination is Los Angeles, assuming both teams win today, and then, if they can sail through that series, it's on to the World Series.

It'll be a cruise worth taking, so come along for the ride. Do I hear everyone climbing aboard?

The Baseball Gods Are Toying With Me, But No More

(Originally posted October 9, 2013)

Up until today, the Baseball Gods, the Lords of Baseball, have been toying with me. Clearly they have decided that 2013 should be the year that they make me look completely and utterly foolish, if not completely ignorant of the game and its teams/players.

First, they decimated the already elderly and feeble Yankees with injuries, and then somehow made it seem like Joe Girardi was a great manager, so much so that the team has allegedly offered him a three year, *fifteen million dollar* contract to stay on as skipper despite his obvious (at least to me) deficiencies. And he has not said "yes" yet, because a potentially higher payday may be looming in the Windy City with the lovable Cubbies.

Then, the Baseball Gods convinced me to root for the sentimental underdog, the Pittsburgh Pirates - I posted a blog about my jumping on their band-ship, and what happened? They lost that evening, of course. If they lose Game 5 to the Cardinals, I suspect that the residents of Steel City will be blaming me for the team's misfortune.

So yesterday I thought I could outsmart the Baseball Gods, and wrote a post about how I was rooting for the Red Sox - so that they would suffer from my curse and lose. The result was, sadly, predictable. The Red Sox won, 3-1, and advanced to the American League Championship Series. Ugh.

Well, they will toy with me and my emotions no more. There are currently six teams still alive in the playoffs. As of tomorrow night, there will be four. I will not announce my preferences again. I have been to the stadiums of all six teams, and have jerseys for five of them (I would never, ever wear a Red Sox jersey, of course) so, no matter who advances to the World Series, I can don their colors and act like a fan, should I so choose.

Not that I can't try one more time, though - let's assume I still wanted the Pirates to win - if so, I would have to root for the Cardinals, post some pictures of myself at Busch Stadium, and somehow trick the Baseball Gods into thinking that I was being sincere, unlike yesterday, obviously.

(pause so that I can put my plan into action)

How great would it be for the Cardinals to return to the World Series? Another of baseball's storied franchises - Stan Musial, Lou Brock, Bob Gibson, Ozzie Smith, et al. ruled the National League at times, if memory serves, they have the most World Series victories of any National League team. Also, until baseball expanded to California, the team was the favorite, I am told, of all points west of the Mississippi. That means that half of the country was comprised of Cards' fans.

And the new Busch Stadium is great - here are some pictures:

Me in my Cardinals' jersey before the game - it was like a college football game, as the entire stadium was clad in Cardinal Red

The scoreboard, lit up at night

171

With the statue of the great Bob Gibson outside of Busch Stadium.

So I say to the Baseball Gods and Lords of Baseball - here's hoping that tonight, the Birds will fly to victory.

Shhh, don't tell anyone my plan. I haven't jumped ship.

Extra Innings: The Cardinals did defeat the Pirates, and gained entry into the World Series. Unfortunately, they were defeated in the Series by the Boston Red Sox in six games.

Which Players Make Up Baseball's Mount Rushmore?

(Originally posted March 25, 2014)

An article on today's Fox Sports site discusses the attempts at one writer's attempts at creating major league baseball's "Mount Rushmore," presumably the four best or most important players ever. Citing various polls, the decision of the original author is to carve the likenesses of Babe Ruth, Jackie Robinson, Willie Mays, and Ted Williams into the face of the mountain. The writer of the actual article referenced below comes to a (mostly) different conclusion - naming Honus Wagner, Babe Ruth, Satchel Paige, and Cal Ripken.

Naturally, the article got me thinking of which players I would memorialize on such a shrine. Recently, with the retirement of Mariano Rivera and the impending retirement of Derek Jeter, the topic of the Yankees' Mt. Rushmore has been raised - with almost universal results - Babe Ruth, Lou Gehrig, Joe DiMaggio, and Mickey Mantle. Mo and DJ are relegated to the second, lower, carvings - likely along with Yogi Berra and, possibly, Whitey Ford.

But the entire major leagues? That's a tough one, of course. I would start with Jackie Robinson, arguably one of the most important players in history, if not the most important. Babe Ruth seems a lock - the all-time home run king for decades, an excellent pitcher as well as a hitter, and a man who out homered entire teams in the late 1920s. That means that I have half of the sculpture done.

Number three on my list is Hank Greenberg, the man who acted as trailblazer for Jewish players in the same way that Jackie Robinson did for African-Americans. True, there are more African-Americans in major league baseball than Jews (although these days the disparity is not all that great) but the courage and class shown by Greenberg was tremendous, and did open the doors for players like Sandy Koufax, Al Rosen, Shawn Green, Ian Kinsler, and others.

For the final slot, I am going to select Curt Flood. It was Flood's challenge of baseball's "reserve clause" that led, several years later, to the first free agents. The changes to the game which resulted from free agency were the greatest changes since Robinson opened the gates for African-Americans to join the majors. No longer were players locked in to one team for their entire careers. Now, players can shop their services to the highest bidder, creating a culture where loyalty, for the most part, has eroded to the point of being almost non-existent.

As they sing in "Wicked" - "I can't say that I've been changed for the better, but I know I've been changed for good." I'm not saying that free agency is a positive, now, but at the time it served its purpose. Much like some labor unions. And all players owe this "freedom" to Curt Flood.

So my Mt. Rushmore consists, in order of their appearance in the game, of Babe Ruth, Hank Greenberg, Jackie Robinson, and Curt Flood.

Note that if we were choosing based solely on playing ability, I would amend to Ruth, Willie Mays, Koufax, and Gehrig.

Extra Innings: I am sticking by my selections, but thought I would share some of the players named in the comments made to the original blog post: Ted Williams, Ty Cobb, Roberto Clemente, Barry Bonds, Warren Spahn, Pete Rose, Cy Young, Hank Aaron, Tom Seaver, and Walter Johnson. You really cannot argue with any of these players being included, other than for drug-related reasons. Speaking of steroids ...

The funniest comment was this one: "Since Mount Rushmore is high I choose Barry Bonds, Roger Clemens, Mark McGwire and Alex Rodriguez."

Celebrating Hank Aaron's #715, Forty Years Later

(Originally published April 8, 2014)

Every April, Major League Baseball recognizes and honors its first African-American player, Jackie Robinson. On April 15, every baseball player takes the field with the number 42 emblazoned across his back, the number worn by Jackie during his time with the Brooklyn Dodgers. Initially this tribute was begun by a few of the game's African-Americans, but now all players participate and the number 42 has been retired by major league baseball – and with Mariano Rivera's retirement last year, no active player will ever again wear number 42.

Today, however, marks the anniversary of an event which also marked tremendous strides in the advancement of African-Americans and the National Pastime. Forty years ago today, on April 8, 1974, the Braves' Hank Aaron launched home run number 715, breaking the all-time home run record which had been held by Babe Ruth for almost four decades. Many records in baseball are thought to be "unbreakable" – Joe DiMaggio's 56-game hitting streak, Cy Young's career victory total of 511 among them. For a long time, the Babe's career total of 714 was considered unassailable as well; remember, when the Babe played, he out-homered entire teams in some seasons.

Yet at the end of 1973, Aaron clubbed home run number 713, leaving him one shy of baseball immortality. Number 714 was struck on opening day, in Cincinnati off of the Reds' Jack Billingham (the first pitch he saw in the new season), and then Aaron sat out a game, before being forced to play by then Commissioner Bowie Kuhn, so that he could pass the Babe in the Braves' home park, in front of the teams' fans. On April 8, Aaron stepped to the plate against the Dodgers' Al Downing, who coincidentally, shared Aaron's uniform number 44. In front of a nationwide televised audience, Aaron rose to the occasion, belting number 715.

Aaron's assault on Ruth's hallowed record was met with much of the same animosity that was encountered by Robinson when he broke baseball's color line in 1947. Aaron received bag after bag of hate mail; letters filled with death threats and racial epithets. Similar threats and profanities were spewed at him in stadiums across the country, a veritable concert of racial indignities and calls from those who did not want an African-American player to take the home run crown from the mythical Ruth. Yet Aaron carried on with his quest – quietly, but seething internally, a bitterness which still boils over at times today when Aaron is interviewed.

Tonight, ESPN will be re-enacting the home run, appropriately at 7:15 pm. Presumably, the show will include an interview with Aaron, who will hopefully look back fondly at the chase for Ruth's record, in sharp contrast to the pressure and angst that accompanied his pursuit. As he said recently, "[s]ometimes you think about it, and it was a moment you should have been enjoying yourself. Then you look back, and it wasn't that way, because there were so many other things that were involved in life. All the things that people were talking about, hateful things."

Aaron retired as baseball's all-time home run leader with a total of 755 homers. That total was later surpassed by Barry Bonds, but Bonds' totals were tainted by his purported steroid usage, leaving most fans still believing that "Hammerin' Hank" Aaron is still the all-time king.

There will be celebrations tonight, but baseball can go one step further. Perhaps, on April 8, 2018, the 44th anniversary of the magical home run, all players will honor Aaron by wearing his number 44. Then, the next week, they can dust off their once-a-season number 42 jerseys to honor Jackie Robinson – which seems to be a pretty powerful one-two combination.

Albert Pujols Swats Homer #500 - So Why the Negativity?

(Originally posted April 23, 2014)

Last night, Albert Pujols hit career home runs number 499 and 500, making him the 26th person in major league history to join what was once considered to be the elite "500 Home Run Club". Normally, this would be cause for celebration and for heaping accolades on the Angels' slugging first baseman. Instead, however, the jaded perspectives of baseball, resulting from the inflated statistics of the "Steroid Era", have seemed to minimize what would otherwise be an amazing accomplishment.

This morning, Mike Greenberg and Mike Golic of ESPN radio discussed Pujols' home run, and opined that its importance has been diminished due to the fact that there are now 26 members of the "club," thereby making it less exclusive. They then went on to state that the inclusion in its membership of several known and suspected steroid users further damaged the "elite" status of the group.

Why not, however, view Pujols' accomplishments in a more positive light? Are we doomed to condemn ever player of our generation due to the actions of others? Pujols was the first person to hit 30 or more home runs in each of his first dozen years in the majors and, yes, there were rumors of him using performance-enhancing drugs; those rumors came to a screeching halt, however, in August of 2013 when former slugger Jack Clark accused Albert of using steroids – Albert threatened litigation, Clark recanted his statement, and there have been no allegations since that time which have linked Pujols to any such PED usage.

So let's assume that Pujols is clean – and if so, we should be celebrating home run number 500, not minimizing it due to the action of others. In fact, if we want to consider those tainted players as soiling the elite nature of the club, then why not forget about the fact that Pujols is the 26th person to hit 500 homers, and instead count the number of such sluggers who did so without synthetic assistance?

Mike and Mike also pointed out that there have been eleven people to join the ranks of the 500 since 1999. Of those eleven, however, seven are suspected/accused of using PED's – Mark McGwire (1999), Barry Bonds (2001), Sammy Sosa (2003), Rafael Palmeiro (2003), Alex Rodriguez (2007), Manny Ramirez (2008), and Garry Sheffield (2009). That means that only four "clean" players – Ken Griffey, Jr. (2004), Frank Thomas (2007), Jim Thome (2007) and now Pujols – have swatted home run number 500 since Eddie Murray hit his in 1996. Four new entrants in 18 years? That still seems pretty exclusive to me. And the last member before Murray was Mike Schmidt in 1987 – meaning that only five people have, unaided, joined the club since 1987, a period of 27 years.

Consider this – Ronald Reagan was still President in 1987. That means that this country has had five different Presidents during this same time period.

And if we eliminate the "dirty seven" we are left with a club whose ranks are limited to 19 members – still very exclusive, by any standards. For comparison's sake, the other "exclusive" club in baseball, the pitchers' "300 victory" club, now boasts 24 members – even if we eliminate Roger Clemens due to his steroid use, that still leaves 23, or four more than the clean 500 home run hitters. And the "3,000 hit club?" – there are 28 members of that group. Even if we toss out Palmeiro, for the same reasons as his exclusion from the 500 homer group, that leaves 27 – and eleven of its members have joined since 1987 – making Pujols' achievement in reaching 500 home runs even more special.

So let's forget about the negativity and try to point baseball in a positive direction. While I am not suggesting that we all act like Mark McGwire and simply forget about the past (his mantra from his appearance before Congress regarding steroid use in baseball), that does not mean that we need to stigmatize all players due to the actions of others. Let's celebrate Pujols' blasts from last night –

also made special by the fact that it was the first time that a player reached 500 in a multi-homer game, and the fact that he struck both homers number 400 and 500 in the same stadium, Nationals Ballpark in Washington, DC.

Congratulations, Albert – don't let the naysayers get you down. And if you average 20 homers a year for the next five years, you will join the even more exclusive "600 club" – whose ranks include eight members – but only five of whom did so without steroids. Maybe when you hit that mark, people will simply celebrate the achievement rather than trying to minimize it because of your cheating brethren.

Extra Innings: Boston's David Ortiz joined the exclusive ranks of the "500 club" in September 2015, but I saw no need to celebrate his reaching this accomplishment. Let's just say that I believe he had more than a little pharmaceutical assistance during his career, despite his continued protestations to the contrary. Ortiz recently announced that he would be retiring after the 2016 season. No doubt he will get a "farewell tour" similar to those enjoyed by Mariano Rivera and Derek Jeter. When the Yankees honor him, it will be a sad day, if not the saddest day, in Yankee Stadium history.

One Day in Baseball - The Good, The Bad, and the Ugly

(Originally posted August 31, 2014)

The news reports on the fate of major league baseball are growing direr by the day. Baseball is losing its young fan base, the researchers cry. The dearth of African-American players will be accompanied by an ever-increasing lack of interest in the game from that portion of the population. Football has replaced baseball as the nation's biggest sport.

Baseball, however, still maintains much of its popularity – granted, it is difficult to truly measure baseball against football (despite the overwhelming desires to do so) because baseball is played daily over the course of its six-month season, whereas football is essentially played by each team only one time per week over its four-month season. Whereas football writers must fill their daily columns with injury updates and "human-interest" type stories over the week's period, baseball's writers are blessed with being able to report on the previous night's games, as well as the afore-mentioned injury updates and "human interest" stories on an almost daily (six or seven times per week, for the most part) basis.

Like most other sports, baseball is a game of numbers – there are numerous hallowed records in the annals of major league baseball, some of which will seemingly never be eclipsed – Cy Young's career wins total of 511, Joe DiMaggio's 56-game hitting streak, Pete Rose's all-time best hit total of 4,192, to name a few. Then again, Hank Aaron's 714 career home run record and Mark McGwire's 70 home runs in one season were both considered unassailable until steroid-fueled Barry Bonds shattered both.

An on any given day, something special or newsworthy can take place. Yesterday was one of those days – three separate events, each noteworthy in their

181

own respect – for sake of convenience, let's term them the good, the bad, and the ugly.

The Good: White Sox pitcher Chris Sale struck out 13 Tigers' hitters in Chicago's 6-3 victory over Detroit. In an otherwise meaningless game for Chicago – the team is 14 games under .500 and has no chance of making the playoffs this season – this achievement was special in that it was the 17th time in his career that Sale has struck out ten or more batters in a game; this ties him with Hall of Famer Ed Walsh for the franchise record. Making the feat even more impressive is that Sale has taken only 81 starts to reach this team standard, whereas Walsh started 312 games (almost four times as many games) for the Chi Sox. Couple that with the fact that the team has been in existence for 114 years, and that makes Sale's accomplishment a clear winner for the "good" story of the day.

The Bad: Mets' General Manager Sandy Alderson boldly predicting during Spring Training that his young team would win 90 games (out of a possible 162) this season. Such a record would constitute a 16-win improvement over last year's 74-88 won-loss record, and the proclamation was met with snorts of derision by many, including this writer, especially as the team was to face its 2014 schedule without the ace of last year's staff, Matt Harvey, who was lost for the season due to arm surgery.

Yesterday, Alderson's dreams were officially shattered as the Mets lost to the only team behind them in the standings, the Phillies, leaving their current record at 63-73 and making it mathematically impossible for them to reach 90 victories. Needing eleven victories in their last 26 games just to equal last-year's won-lost mark, the loss yesterday, and the final blow to Alderson's prediction, is the "bad" story of the day.

The Ugly: One of the biggest rivalries in baseball, if not all of sports, is the rivalry between the Yankees and the Red Sox. Acrimony between the two AL East rivals dates back to at least 1919, when cash-strapped Red Sox owner Harry

Frazee sold Babe Ruth to the Yankees to finance his production of the play "No No Nanette," thereby setting into motion the "Curse of the Bambino," a curse which haunted the Sox until it was exorcised in October 2004. The Yankees' faithful boast of their record 27 World Championships. Red Sox nation points to the fact that its team has captured three titles in the last decade. The players on the teams used to hate each other – brawls between them, and animosity between its stars – were commonplace. Now, with free agency and frequent movement of players, the level of animosity has abated to a large extent, but the rabid fan bases of each team still hold the other with contempt.

Yesterday, the Yankees were defeated by the Toronto Blue Jays by a score of 2-0. Toronto hurlers Drew Hutchinson and Aaron Sanchez combined not only to shut out the Yankees, but also held the team to only one hit, a double by Mark Teixeira. At the same time that the Yankees' bats were being stymied in the Great White North, Tampa pitchers Jake Ordozzi, Jeff Beiveau and Kirby Yates were bedeviling and confounding the Red Sox hitters – allowing only a single to Boston's Will Middlebrooks en route to a one-hit, 7-0 victory.

While I have been unable to verify whether or not both of these teams, two of baseball's most storied franchises, have ever been dominated in such a manner on the same day, it appears safe to say that yesterday's joint ineptitude was unprecedented. The joint inability of these teams to muster more than one hit on the same day - especially when one considers that they were dominated by five pitchers who, up until yesterday, were names that I had never even heard - certainly qualifies as the "ugly" story.

*****

And remember, there will be a whole new set of "good," "bad," and "ugly" today – perhaps another record will be set, another special performance that will be talked about for years to come, or a team will accomplish something that it never had before. That's the beauty of baseball, and why the sport will survive, and thrive, despite the dire predictions as illustrated in the beginning to this post.

As James Earl Jones so eloquently stated in "Field of Dreams" – *"The one constant through all the years, Ray, has been baseball. America has rolled by like an army of steamrollers. It has been erased like a blackboard, rebuilt and erased again. But baseball has marked the time. This field, this game: it's a part of our past, Ray. It reminds us of all that once was good and that could be again."*

Extra Innings: I believe it was Joe DiMaggio who said that he played 100% every game because he did not want to disappoint the fan who came only to that game, the gist being that there were people in the stands every day who were not regular visitors to the stadium, and that specific game may have been the only time in their lives that they were able to see the Great DiMaggio in person. Every day brings its own good, bad, and ugly. It is for that reason that, even though each team plays 162 games over a long, six-month stretch, each game is, in its own way, important. I have borne witness to the good (sometimes the great), the bad, and, most definitely, the ugly. And I keep going back for more ... because you never know when you will see something truly special.

The Idiocy of Baseball's Statistics and Players

(Originally posted October 29, 2014)

Tonight, the Kansas City Royals and San Francisco Giants square off in Game 7 of the 2014 World Series. With the series tied at three games apiece, the winner of tonight's game will be crowned 2014 World Series Champions.

The big question, of course, is who will win? Well, if you read some of the statistics being thrown around, there really is no debate:

Fact #1 – The Giants have never won a winner-take-all game (like a Game 7) in the World Series.

Fact #2 – The Royals have only played in Game 7 of a post-season series twice, and have won both times.

Clearly, therefore, the Giants are chokers and the Royals have ice running through their veins - so Kansas City will definitely win tonight, right?

Not so fast. Both of these statistics are, at best, ludicrous – because they have no relationship whatsoever to the current teams, or, realistically, to any of the players on either the Giants' or Royals' 2014 rosters.

The last time that the Giants lost a World Series in seven games was in 2002, a dozen years ago, when they were beaten by the Anaheim Angels. Not one of the current Giants played in the 2002 World Series. Only a select few were even in the major leagues in 2002.

The time before that was when the Giants were beaten in seven games by the New York Yankees in 1962. None of the current Giants' players were even born at the time.

185

As for the Royals, the last time they won a Game 7 was in the 1985 World Series, over the St. Louis Cardinals. None of the current Kansas City players was playing at the time (it was 29 years ago) and only eleven members of the current 25-man roster were even alive on the day that Game 7 was played. The team's elder statesman, Jason Frasor, was all of eight years old when that Game 7 ended.

I think it is safe to say, therefore, that these statistics have no bearing on tonight's game.

The stat about tonight's SF starter, Tim Hudson, having an Earned Run Average above 5.00 for his last few starts? That is a statistic that might bear some consideration, and could weigh in favor of a good night for the Royals' faithful, especially after last night's romp in Game 6. Then again, the Giants can pull all-time World Series great Madison Bumgarner, and his career 0.29 World Series ERA, out of the bullpen to pitch tonight (as the 2001 Arizona Diamondbacks did against the Yankees with Randy Johnson) so anything can happen.

The home team is 9-0 in the last nine Game 7s. Some might think that this statistic is dispositive – unless the majority of the players who will be seeing action tonight have played in those nine games, however, I would beg to differ.

*****

As for player idiocy, I should clarify that I am referring to a former player. Apparently former A's slugger Jose Canseco shot himself in the hand while cleaning what he mistakenly thought was an unloaded gun. The blast severed his middle finger. Now he won't be able to properly respond to his detractors. His girlfriend took to Twitter and posted a request that people should "[p]lease pray for his finger!!"

Sorry, honey, but some of us have better things to do. Like watching Game 7 tonight – because I don't know who is going to win. That's why they play the game.

Extra Innings: As I thought, you could have simply thrown all of the statistics away. The Giants won Game 7 by a 3-2 count. As predicted above, San Francisco did pull ace Madison Bumgardner out of the bullpen, and he responded with a game for the ages, throwing five innings of shutout ball to cement the Giants' victory. But shed no tears for Kansas City, who roared back with a stellar 2015 campaign, culminating in the team capturing the World Series championship in a five-game series with the New York Mets.

Baseball's 2015 Fiscal Imprudence Has Already Begun

(Originally posted November 17, 2014)

The 2015 baseball season is still months away, but as a bitter cold grips a large part of the United States, it seems to be a good time to begin looking forward to the summer game, and to turn our attention to what is shaping up to be an off-season of large contracts and, based on what we have seen thus far, fiscal imprudence.

Already, the pundits in the New York area are guessing as to which large-ticket free agents will ink mega-contracts with the Yankees for 2015 and beyond. Big-time pitchers like Jon Lester and Max Scherzer are the names being bandied about to help stabilize a feeble and questionable pitching staff, and it is evident that the team still requires a power hitter to properly compete in the suddenly competitive American League East.

And when the Yankees throw their money around, many will urge, it will be done imprudently and the team will then be bogged down with aging players making excessive amounts of money for extended periods of time. A look at the current roster shows at least three aging veterans, still under contract for at least a few more years, at salaries far beyond their current worth – CC Sabathia, Mark Teixeira, and baseball's returning "bad boy," Alex Rodriguez.

Still, the Yankees cannot be considered to be the only team foolish enough to burden itself with a cast of aging, overpriced, and underperforming veterans. In fact, three such examples of possible imprudence have filled the news reports over the past few days:

Name	Team	Contract term
AJ Burnett	*Pittsburgh Pirates*	*One year, $8.5 million*
Victor Martinez	*Detroit Tigers*	*Four years, $68 million*
Giancarlo Stanton	*Miami Marlins*	*13 years, $325 million*

Let's address these in order –

AJ Burnett   Burnett is a career 155-150 pitcher over his sixteen-year career, during which he has toiled for five different teams. His biggest career move was pitching brilliantly against the Yankees while he was on the Toronto Blue Jays, leading the team in the Bronx to mistakenly sign him to a long-term, ridiculously high contract at the same time that the team inked their other double-initialed hurler, the afore-mentioned CC Sabathia. While Sabathia paid dividends for several years, however, Burnett did the opposite. Following one good season (2009), in which he did help the team win the World Series, things went south quickly for Burnett. In 2010, he sported an Earned Run Average of 5.26, one of the highest ever for a starting pitcher, and the highest ever for a Yankees' starting pitcher.

He was unceremoniously shipped off to Pittsburgh, where he pitched for two seasons before spurning their new contract offer for a richer contract in Philadelphia. Last year, he thrilled the City of Brotherly love to the tune of an 8-18 record; his 18 losses leading the league, before turning down a $12 million offer to return. He has now re-signed with Pittsburgh, and one can only wonder why a team which made the playoffs would spend so much for an average pitcher who will be 38 years old when the 2015 season begins.

Victor Martinez   Martinez capped off a stellar 2014 season by finishing second in the American League MVP voting, losing to unanimous winner Mike Trout. In 2014, he slugged a career-high 32 home runs, knocked in 103 runs, and batted .335, his highest career average when playing a full season. It's the perfect time for him to sign a lucrative, multi-year contract, right?

For the player, absolutely. For the team, maybe not. Martinez will turn 36 years old days before Christmas, which means that this contract will take him into his 40's. Such an extended contract is dangerous when discussing any player, but seems especially true when discussing Martinez, who has had several injuries during his career and missed the entire 2012 season due to injury. Sandwiching that lost 2012 season were seasons with home run totals of 12 (in 2011) and 14 (in 2013). The one-time catcher is now primarily a Designated Hitter, which should spare his body a great deal of wear-and-tear, but the odds tell us that a four-year contract is too long for his services.

Giancarlo Stanton   The slugger formerly known as Mike also finished second in the MVP voting this year, as Stanton was the runner-up in the National League balloting to Dodgers' pitcher Clayton Kershaw. Stanton ran roughshod over league pitching in 2014, belting 37 home runs and knocking in 105 runs before a pitch to his face sidelined him for the season's final couple of weeks. He has averaged almost 31 homers per season over his five-year career, and is expected to eventually retire as one of the game's all-time great sluggers. Many observers have said that he hits the ball harder than any other major leaguer.

Reports indicate that Stanton and the Marlins have finalized a 13-year, $325 million contract. Yes, you read that right – Thirteen years. Three hundred and twenty five million dollars. Earlier reports also indicated that the contract would contain a no-trade clause, as well as an opt-out option for Stanton. He could, therefore, have complete control over how long he actually remains with the Marlins.

Three hundred and twenty five million dollars.

A contract which averages $25 million per year for one of the game's premier sluggers? On its face, it does not seem so outlandish – but what sets this contract apart, of course, is its length. When the 13-year contract expires, Stanton will be 37, and likely not so beastly anymore. Historically, the teams that have signed sluggers to decade-long deals have done so with the belief that the last few years would not likely be productive (Rodriguez's last 10-year deal with the Yankees is a prime example, as was Albert Pujols' contract with the Angels), so one can only wonder what the Marlins would be expecting for the second half of such a deal.

Thirteen years is a really long time.

Think about it. A Jewish son born today will have his Bar Mitzvah during the term of this contract. A child now in kindergarten will graduate from High School before this deal expires. Many things can happen over such an extended period of time – injuries, of course, being the primary concern. The aging process may take its toll on Stanton; diminishing of bat speed and reduction in power are viable possibilities as well.

Simply put, there is a great deal of uncertainty involved with such a contract, such that one must wonder if locking Stanton up for such an extended period of time is a good idea for the Marlins.

*****

The above signings almost make the Mets' recent signing of outfielder Michael Cuddyer to a two-year, $21 million contract seem cheap. Then again, he did miss over 100 games last year so there is uncertainty as to his possible productivity.

Soon, the inevitable will take place. The Yankees will sign a big-name free agent, possibly one of the two star pitchers noted above. The contract will be for somewhere between five and ten years, and the likelihood is that it will be in the $200 million range. And the also inevitable calls of protest will begin – people will complain that the Yankees are again trying to buy a championship, and that they are ruining the game with their excessive spending.

To the contrary, I will urge. Based on the contracts discussed above, I will counter with the argument that they are just keeping up with the Joneses. Or the Stantons.

Extra Innings: Burnett started the year well, pitching at a high level through the All-Star break, and was selected to the All-Star game. He finished the season with a respectable 9-7 won-loss record, along with a 3.18 ERA in 26 starts. One could easily argue that he was worth the value of his contract.

Martinez played in only 120 games in 2015. His final statistics for the season were 11 Home Runs, 64 RBI, and a .245 batting average. Thus far, he has not earned the money being paid to him under the new contract.

Stanton was simply awesome … when he played. He appeared in only 74 games, slightly more than half a season, and during that abbreviated time smacked 27 home runs and knocked in 67. Over a full season, these numbers translate to 59 homers and 147 RBI. If only he can stay healthy for the next five or six years, he will be worth the millions being paid to him.

You Cannot Look Forward Without Looking Back (Sorry, MLB)

(Originally posted February 6, 2015)

I am one of the holdouts who still reads newspapers. I do not like to obtain my news in the snippet, sound-bite formats which populate the internet, and instead prefer the feel of actual paper, reading actual newsprint, in the morning. The unfortunate reality is that much of the news is of a negative nature, and I can offer today's local paper as evidence – three of the four articles on the front page of today's *Newark Star-Ledger* are what I would term "negative" (or sad) news:

1.   Some time ago, a four year-old boy shot his six year-old playmate with a loaded gun which had been left unattended by his father. Yesterday, the father was sentenced to three years in jail for leaving the gun accessible to his young son.

2.   The football coach of Sayreville High School was officially relieved of his duties in the wake of the hazing scandal, involving allegations of sexual abuse among the players, which rocked the central NJ town last fall.

3.   NBC anchor Brian Williams is being vilified by veterans after it was revealed that he has been lying about being aboard a war-time helicopter that was struck by enemy fire.

There is a picture of the puppy from the latest Budweiser commercial with a teaser for an article on page 22, but that picture alone is certainly not enough to defray the negativity which pervades the front page.

Yet, the "saddest" sentence which appears in today's paper has nothing to do with any of the above articles. It is a sentence which appears on page 31 of the paper, on the third page of the sports section, and while the article in which it appears deals with major league baseball, the subject matter of the article, and this sentence, have societal ramifications which reach well beyond the baseball diamond. The article in question focuses on the new MLB Commissioner, Robert Manfred, and the attempts that the sport will be making to reach out to a wider and younger audience. The average baseball fan is now 55 years old, according to the story, up from 41 a decade ago – and the sport's representatives continue to fret about how to engage the youth of this country – to preserve interest in what was the "national pastime".

The sentence which sent shudders up my spine?

"If their grandparents want to share stories of watching Sandy Koufax pitch for the Los Angeles Dodgers, so much the better, but baseball's new pitch does not rely on the nostalgia that long has been one of the game's primary selling points."

The Lords of Baseball, however, cannot simply forsake the past in order to engage people in the present and future. The history of baseball, the stories of its past, are what make the game, the culture of the game, so interesting and integral to the growth of this country. One needs only to consider James Earl Jones' soliloquy in "Field of Dreams," about how baseball is the one constant of this country, to appreciate the importance of its past. Part of the league's efforts at expanding its fan base, for years now, has been focused on attempting to increase interest among African-American youth. Any such efforts, however, cannot focus only on phone apps and glitzy internet pages – the efforts look back to the past. They must include retelling the stories of Jackie Robinson's courageous efforts at breaking baseball's "color line" in 1947 and becoming the first African-American player in the major leagues. Any such efforts must include discussions of major league baseball's pre-eminent African-American players from the 1950's and 1960's, including Frank Robinson, Willie Mays, Hank Aaron, and, of course, the recently deceased Ernie Banks. They can also focus on the current crop of players, of course, but to not continue to glorify the trailblazers does those all-time greats a disservice.

Not only to engage youth, mind you, but it is also critical that the current players should be well-versed on those who ran the basepaths or stood on the mound before them – I would be willing to wager that a scant few current players were aware of the career statistics of Ernie Banks, one of baseball's last great ambassadors, who died last month. The lack of knowledge of the game's history by its players detracts not only from the game itself, but also from having people gain interest in the sport – so if the MLB does focus only on the now, and in so doing forgets the past, it will be making a big mistake.

I would also be remiss if I did not point out another critical part of the above-quoted sentence: the inclusion of only one player's name – Sandy Koufax – a player whose name is still spoken in hushed tones among baseball historians, Koufax is inarguably on any pundit's shortlist of all-time great starting pitchers. The statistics that he put together in the mid-1960's remain the bellwether for any discussion of dominance over a multi-year stretch, such as all of the recent conversations regarding fellow Dodger pitcher Clayton Kershaw.

More importantly, however, Koufax is regarded as the greatest Jewish baseball player ever to don a uniform. The inclusion of his name in a sentence regarding discussions between grandparents and grandchildren, therefore, is ironic, if not completely appropriate. Think about it. It is eerily reminiscent of one of the most critical issues facing the Jewish people today – the rise of anti-Semitism (on this blog site and across the globe) and the near-extinction of the survivors and witnesses to the atrocity of the Holocaust. Young Jewish children are encouraged to "twin" with a Holocaust survivor, so that the elder can tell stories of the savagery of the Nazis, such that the stories will "live on" with the younger generation and will continue to be told for generations to come.

If the stories cease, it is believed, then the memories will eventually cease as well – and the naysayers will continue to grow in strength and number. Anti-Semitism continues to exist in great numbers; incredibly, there are also still those people who deny that the Holocaust took place, or seek to somehow minimize the number of Jews who were eliminated during that period – six million Jewish lives were lost to the Nazi death camps – and the number of future lives, those who would have been born of those killed by Hitler's troops, is immeasurable. "Never Forget" is what is said, and an entire religion is making an effort to ensure that this mantra is followed.

Clearly, I am not comparing the importance of remembering the Holocaust with the comparatively less important need for baseball to remember its past. The concept of "Never Forget", however, does apply in both cases. It is critical for the Jewish people to remember those who perished in the Holocaust – as it is said; we need to remember "L'dor va dor" – from generation to generation.

The same is true for major league baseball. Statues of former major leaguer and Hall of Famer Roberto Clemente, for example, are all over his homeland of Puerto Rico. No doubt every child on that island, especially those who dream of playing major league baseball, knows of Clemente and his importance to the game. There is no reason why the youth of this country cannot be similarly educated. Grandparents need to keep telling their grandchildren about baseball's heyday. Without such conversations, the sport will never again rise to the level of importance that it held in the past.

Extra Innings: The great Satchel Paige famously said, "Don't look back, something might be gaining on you." Clearly I disagree. We need to continue to celebrate baseball's past, revel in the memory of its glory days. And now some of you are thinking to yourselves, "spoken like a true Yankees' fan." Perhaps you are correct.

My Curt Schilling Love/Hate Meter is Back to Love

(Originally posted March 5, 2015)

For the better part of a decade and a half now, I have had what I will call a Love/Hate relationship with former pitcher Curt Schilling. More appropriately, I would term it a Respect/Hate relationship. As a Yankees' fan, the specifics of the dichotomy of my feelings for him have been relatively easy to quantify:

Respect

1.   He named his son Gehrig, after Yankee all-time great Lou Gehrig;

2.   He played clean, and had no problem with calling out the steroid users – including testifying as such before Congress;

3.   He is never afraid to "tell it like it is" now as a commentator, and his candor is refreshing;

4.   216 career victories and over 3,100 strikeouts evidence a very nice baseball career;

5.   The "bloody sock" game – pitching through that pain took guts.

Hate

1.   He dominated the Yankees in the 2001 World Series for the Diamondbacks, capturing co-MVP honors for the series with Randy Johnson;

2.   He dominated the Yankees in the 2004 playoffs with the Red Sox, including beating them in the "bloody sock" game;

3.   The "bloody sock" game – enough about it, already.

Last week, however, the "relationship" reached new heights – on the positive side – when he called out two guys who had posted completely vile and hateful things about his daughter on twitter – Schilling had tweeted how proud he was of her regarding a college acceptance, and these two Neanderthals took it upon themselves to reply in a vulgar, completely unacceptable way – and Schilling did not take these comments lightly, exposing the two and their comments – and now, one has lost his job and one has been suspended from his college.

By the way, the fact that both men are from my home state of New Jersey and that one worked for the Yankees makes this story even more reprehensible to me, lest anyone believe that the comments of these two idiots at all reflect the beliefs of all New Jersey residents or those who work with the Bronx Bombers. Thankfully, they do not.

All too often, hatred rules the internet – this is especially true when people feel that they are impervious to ramifications, such as when they post using assumed names – and it is about time that someone did something about it. It is a shame that Schilling had to take these measures in response to what started as a nice fatherly post about his daughter, but if even one internet troll thinks twice about making such comments in the future, then Schilling has again earned my respect – and no matter how much they talk about that damned bloody sock in the future, my respect for him will not wane.

As Schilling said, echoing his disdain for PED users in baseball, "It's like the performance-enhancing stuff in baseball. If you did it once, you might have made a bad decision. But this is a conscious effort and a conscious decision to be really evil."

Score one for the good guys.

CHAPTER 7 – LEGAL ISSUES, SUCH AS DOMESTIC VIOLENCE AND RACISM (including other sports)

NFL Avoids Being Tackled By the Seau Family's Litigation

(Originally posted January 25, 2013)

It seems that Junior Seau's uncanny ability to make the "big hit" on opposing ball carriers was not passed on to his family or its attorneys. News came Wednesday that Seau's family had filed litigation against the NFL, blaming it for Junior's suicide. The former star linebacker committed suicide last May, and examination of his brain revealed that he suffered from chronic traumatic encephalopathy (CTE), presumably from the untold number of hits to the head that he sustained while playing football. The litigation, in part, accuses the NFL of both ignoring and concealing evidence of the risks associated with traumatic brain injuries.

Much will be likely written about this suit in the coming months - what the NFL did and did not know regarding such injuries, what the NFL has done to prevent such injuries going forward, about the thousands of other suits currently pending against the NFL, and about the players and their willingness to risk such injuries. Thousands of documents will be exchanged, which may show that the NFL knew of and/or buried certain evidence of head injuries, and which may also show that the player's association and/or players had greater knowledge of the risks than we have been led to believe thus far.

As a fan who has watched NFL games during fall and winter weekends for four decades, it seems obvious that there is an element of violence which, inevitably, will lead to long-term traumatic injuries. Importantly, there are also countless practices in which these players have participated. Before their NFL careers, they played and practiced in college. They played and practiced in High

School. They likely played in Pop Warner or some other youth organization. And, no doubt, they played "pick-up" games with their friends without wearing helmets, pads, or any other forms of protection. So how many hits have they taken? It is impossible to determine. "Thousands" likely does not even begin to describe the number.

Today's players are, for the most part, bigger than the players of yesteryear. They are stronger and faster. The field, however, is still the same size, and the NFL is cramming larger, stronger, and faster players into the same 100-yard field. The collisions are more fierce, the playing (artificial) surfaces harder than when football first began, and, as a result, the potential for injury is much greater – no matter what type of padding you place inside of a player's helmet.

As an attorney, I expect to hear terms that are thrown about in personal injury cases – defenses to the litigation will include *"assumption of the risk", "contributory negligence", "comparative negligence",* and so forth. The plaintiffs will argue *"willful concealment"* of information and that the NFL, in order to protect its own *"bottom line"*, purposefully exposed its players to injury.

In this case, however, the cynic in me offers potentially the greatest perspective – why now? Why was the litigation filed during the week before the Super Bowl? Without knowing California law, I think it is safe to assume that the Statute of Limitations for such cases is not eight months, so there was no need for the Seau family to rush to the courthouse and file other than to maximize their publicity during the hype-crazy period prior to the sport's biggest game. On that basis alone, I am skeptical.

What is the purpose of the litigation? Is it to further efforts at making the NFL games safer for its current players, or is it merely to seek monetary recovery for the Seau family? Note that I use the word "merely" very carefully here. The

Seau family will no doubt argue the deprivation of millions of dollars of income due to Junior's death, for he could have been a coach, a commentator, or done something else connected with the sport which could have led to a large payday. And that may be true. But – no doubt Junior Seau made millions of dollars during his career. As a result, the family should still be in possession of millions of dollars, such that they *do not need* the additional fortunes. If all of the money is gone, then the NFL is not to blame for their current situation. They can blame Junior (or themselves) if it was all spent, or his financial advisors if the monies were not invested properly.

Simply put, in this economy, where people continue to struggle to put food on the table despite working harder than ever, I find it difficult to believe that the American public will feel pity for the Seau family if they do not reap additional millions of dollars from the NFL and the other defendants.

If this sounds cruel, I apologize.

Also, that Junior Seau knew the dangers associated with playing football for so long simply cannot be ignored. He played in the NFL for 20 years. He spent his entire professional life (and his high school and college lives, etc) hurtling his body at other players in an effort to maximize his impact with them and knock them to the ground. According to reports, the suit essentially acknowledges his understanding of its dangers, quoting him from the 1993 "NFL Rocks" as saying: *"if I can feel some dizziness, I know that guy is feeling double."* These are not the words of someone who did not understand that injury can result from his playing the sport.

There is also an element of the unknown that any *reasonable person* (another legal term) should be able to appreciate. A man who propels himself, sometimes headfirst, into other large people and intends to knock both himself and the other to the hard artificial turf must know that there may be some repercussions.

People often ask what happens if I eat something with gluten in it – as I suffer from Celiac Disease – I explain that I would likely become ill, and then feel sluggish for the next couple of days, which has happened when I inadvertently ate something gluten-y in the past. I add, however, that my real fear is the unknown. I am more afraid of the potential long-term effects of gluten intake, especially when the effects are insidious and I may not know the full ramifications until years later.

Is it wrong to assume that Junior Seau, or other NFL players, are capable of thinking the same way? Or do the paycheck and glory simply trump these concerns?

We often hear these players described as "warriors". We hear how players who have sustained concussions want to still go out there and play, because that is their mentality. And this is glorified by those who have played the game – the "warrior" is exulted by his teammates and coaches, and the person who takes himself out of a game (e.g., Jay Cutler) is vilified. I cringed when I watched Robert Griffin III's knee buckle during a recent playoff game. His coach was harangued for keeping him in the game when his health, and, most importantly, long-term NFL career prospects, were in jeopardy. Yet, if Coach Shanahan had taken Griffin out, over Griffin's objection, a Redskins' loss would have led to further ire from the Washington faithful. *It is, to a certain extent, a no-win situation.*

The NFL is currently in such a no-win situation. When it tries to protect its players, the very players whom it is trying to protect cry that it is unfair, that the game is being ruined. Defensive players complain that the quarterbacks are being coddled. They complain about their inability to hit receivers, the so-called "defenseless receivers". At the same time, however, ex-players have filed a mountain of litigations against the league, claiming that it did not do enough to protect them from injury. The Seau litigation is merely the latest thrown on top of the pile, yet it may prove to be the most publicized due to Junior Seau's stature as a player as well as the fact that he did not simply die, but, rather, he committed suicide, just like several before him, including, most recently, Dave Duerson and Ray Easterling.

Sometimes, however, the need to blame others must, inevitably, lead back home. We must take responsibility for our own actions. Here, it is different because the player in question is no longer here, and it is his family who has brought the litigation. It may be hard for them to prove that the NFL caused his suicide. It could have been the thousands of hits sustained before his NFL career that caused his CTE. It could have been actions outside of his playing in the NFL. And, of course, his "assumption of the risk" and "contributory" or "comparative" negligence in continuing to play, even after he began to exhibit signs of irrationality, according to his own family, will also be a factor for the court and/or jury to decide.

It has been opined that suicide is either the greatest form of cowardice and selfishness, or that it is truly the act of a desperate person who sees no other feasible alternative. I make no opinions as to that here. But the cynic in me, the attorney in me, and, yes, the fan in me, all draw the same conclusion. The NFL was not responsible for Junior Seau's suicide. Nor was the helmet maker, or the teams with which he achieved his glory on the gridiron. The person responsible for Junior Seau's suicide was Junior Seau. No amount of money, to his family or anyone else, can ease the pain of his loss, and no amount of money can avoid the conclusion that he caused his own death, the very definition of "suicide".

The fact that the litigation was filed, to me, is sad. The fact that it was filed this week, timed to be publicized on the eve of football's greatest game, a game that Junior Seau had the good fortune to enjoy with two different teams, is sadder. It could have detracted from the game, but, as the media attention about the litigation seems to have already ebbed, only two days later, perhaps the media-attention seeking litigants and counsel have misplayed their hands. We can only hope.

So, the players are able to focus on preparing for the Super Bowl, the Har-bowl, or whatever else you want to call it. These players are preparing to reach the height of their careers with a victory, as well as, perhaps unwittingly, add to the litany of collisions and hits which may lead to long-term disease and/or difficulties.

And they all know it. Junior Seau knew it. We all know it. One of the big criticisms of the baseball players who took steroids to improve their game was that they were potentially sacrificing their long-term health. How is that different from *any* football player who straps on pads and walks onto the football field?

Overtime: **Realistically, what else can you add to this? The debate about football and concussions can go on for pages, if not chapters. The league says that it is trying to address the issue – and every time a new rule is put into place that protects the players' health, there is a backlash about how the league is stifling the defense's abilities to play. Meanwhile, kids continue to practice and play all year long, butting heads with each other and slamming each other to the grass or artificial turf, and the long-term ramifications of these collisions and impacts continue to grow.**

Interestingly, the U.S. Soccer Federation recently announced that players aged 10 and under would be banned from heading the ball, in order to prevent concussions. This decision resulted from a settlement reached in a class action suit brought by youth players against youth soccer groups. Additionally, players aged 11 through 13 would be restricted by the length of practices and number of headers per week. While this was hailed by many, as you might expect, there was also a public outcry from those parents who claim that their children are capable of heading the ball properly and that

their children's abilities to properly excel at the sport have been stymied by this rule.

The lords of sport simply cannot win when it comes to any argument regarding concussions or long-term brain injuries.

Racism and the Ironically-Named Mr. Incognito

(Originally posted November 5, 2013)

There is an extremely disturbing story brewing in Miami and the National Football League, a scenario where the bullying that has been such a hot topic in schools and colleges across this country has now manifested itself among adults, among those perceived to be the biggest and strongest members of our society - professional football players. Jonathan Martin of the Miami Dolphins, a second-year player, fled the team days ago after what was reported to be a bullying incident in the team's cafeteria.

Initially, reports were that Martin had left the team to seek help (read: rehabilitation or therapy) for personal reasons. The obvious implication was that the problem was Martin's, whether it be drug-related, depression-related, or otherwise psychological. Since that time, however, more information has been leaked, and it now appears as if Martin was not just bullied out of Miami, but that he was also threatened and made the subject of bias attacks.

*in·cog·ni·to: With one's identity disguised or concealed... **1.** One whose identity is disguised or concealed; **2.** The condition of having a disguised or concealed identity (taken from freedictionary.com)*

Dolphins' offensive lineman Richie Incognito has been identified as the "ringleader" of the attacks on Martin. Voice mail messages and texts from Incognito, in which he threatens Martin and calls him various slurs, including the forbidden "n" word, have been revealed. It is alleged that Martin actually feared for his safety – due to Incognito. The ironically-named Incognito, therefore, has unwittingly become the face of both rookie hazing and hatred/bigotry.

The Dolphins have suspended Incognito. Whether that suspension will be long-lasting, or whether he will be re-activated to play for the surprisingly playoff-contending team, is yet to be seen. Much will likely depend on how much more information is revealed, and, of course, whether the NFL Players' Association decides to act to protect its member.

There is a certain intrigue to the fact that this soap opera is playing out now, as voters go to the polls across this country to elect the legislators who, presumably, will help shape the United States' path for years to come. This could be the day that the "tea party" begins to be essentially nullified, depending on the outcome of one or more gubernatorial races. It could also be the day that certain rising stars in each political party secure their current positions, as well as place themselves squarely in the running for bigger posts in the future. Of course, there are those who believe that the outcomes of today's elections will have little effect on our future, and that the system is simply so broken that it will continue to degenerate regardless of who is sitting in Washington DC or the various statehouses.

The Martin/Incognito story is one that will dominate the airwaves for some time, as more and more information is revealed about the culture underlying professional sports, about the hazing perpetrated on rookies in the NFL, and, sadly, the racism that continues to pervade not only sports, but our society as a whole. Many will use it as a referendum to stop hazing, not just in sports, not just at college fraternities, but in any societal group.

Many will use it as a message to be sent against racism, but the reality is that bigotry is still pervasive – we see it manifested in many ways, whether it be in the form of racism, anti-Semitism, or anti-homosexual slurs or positions. Newspapers are rife with reports of each, and, as some of us are all too acutely aware, examples of racism and anti-Semitism continue to be found within the very pages of this blog site.

I will leave such broad-brush positions to the pundits. Rather, I will keep my conclusion to a much more basic level - There are thousands of athletes in this country, and over the world, who possess the God-given ability to play professional sports. Just because they have that talent, however, does not mean that they should be given the opportunity to play such games at a professional level. Playing professional sports is not a God-given right. It is a privilege, especially in light of the millions of dollars paid to many of these athletes. It is a privilege that can, and at times, should, be taken away.

The Commissioners and administrators of professional sports are often stymied when they seek to take moral positions. The Players' Associations are so strong, especially in baseball and football, that any action taken by the lords of sport are quickly met with retaliatory actions by the players – witness the football players' continued and inexplicable resistance to safety measures being taken by the NFL, even in the face of their predecessors' litigation against the league for concussions and other head trauma caused during their playing days. Witness the biggest soap opera to hit New York or baseball in some time, the continued saga of Alex Rodriguez and his fight to overturn his drug-related suspension.

It is true that in each of these situations, the leagues reaped the benefits of the delineated transgressions *(football rose to prominence based largely on the ESPN-highlight friendly savagery of its players, some would argue, and there is little doubt that baseball rebounded from its strike-ridden past on the coattails of steroid-juiced monsters like Mark McGwire and Sammy Sosa)* but that does not mean that they cannot take actions now to try to right those wrongs, especially for the protection of the players.

Here, the suspension of Richie Incognito was deemed by the Dolphins to be, presumably, for the protection of both Jonathan Martin and any other players who have been or who would have been subject to his harassment. Incognito appears to be a racist, based on his actions. He also appears to have the need to belittle those below him, like rookies, also based on his actions and various quotes attributed to him in the past. There have been several players penalized, suspended, and fined over the years for taking actions against Incognito on the playing field – which, it may be safe to assume, could have been based on his racist comments. Clearly the man has issues.

Richie Incognito, born in my home state of New Jersey, stands 6 foot 3 inches tall and weighs about 320 pounds. Last year, he was selected to the Pro Bowl for his efforts on the field, and, perhaps in a further note of irony, was co-winner of the "Good Guy" award, which is awarded by NFL writers to a player (or players) on each team. Now, however, he finds himself at the center of a situation completely of his own doing, and one for which he may be banned from football forever.

Richie Incognito forgot one thing while he was harassing Jonathan Martin. There is no God-given right to be able to play professional football.

Overtime: An investigation commissioned by the NFL found that Incognito and others were guilty of bullying Martin; they were also accused of bullying another offensive lineman and two coaches. Incognito now plays with Buffalo, and is being hailed as one of the best offensive lineman of the 2015 season.

Martin was traded to the San Francisco 49ers prior to the 2014 season. He started one game for the 49ers, and was waived prior to the 2015 season. The Carolina Panthers claimed him off of waivers in March of 2015, but Martin retired at the end of July, opting to forego back surgery that would have kept him out of action for the entire season. In August 2015 he penned a Facebook post in which he stated that he had attempted suicide. From the post: "Your job leads you to attempt to kill yourself on multiple occasions. Your self-perceived social inadequacy dominates your every waking moment & thought. You're petrified of going to work. You either sleep 12, 14, 16 hours a day when you can, or not at all. You drink too much, smoke weed constantly, have trouble focusing on doing your job, playing the sport you grew up obsessed with. But one day, you realize how absurd your current mindset is, that this shit doesn't matter. People don't matter. Money doesn't matter. Game and notoriety sure as hell don't matter. Nothing matters besides your family, a few close friends, and your own personal happiness."

Martin's post also described his efforts at being "cool" and not being the "weird kid who acts white", clearly indicating that his inner turmoil existed long before he met Richie Incognito. The acts of bullying that he endured were simply the final straw in his downward spiral. In the law, however, we learn about the "eggshell plaintiff" – that you take the plaintiff as you find him – so even if the injury caused by your actions was worse due to the person's prior condition, you are still responsible. Incognito was told by the coaches that Martin was soft and that he needed to be toughened up. None of them realized that Martin was apparently already well-aware of the perception that he would need to toughen up, but his teammates' efforts at achieving this result had exactly the opposite result.

Another New York Athlete Leaves, Claims He Was Disrespected

(Originally posted March 15, 2014)

And for the second time, I am not shedding any tears for him.

Late last year, former Yankees' second baseman Robinson Cano fled the Big Apple for the Emerald City, signing a contract to play baseball with the Seattle Mariners for the princely sum of $240 million dollars over a ten-year contract term. As he exited, he chastised the Yankees' brass, claiming that their contract offer - of seven years, $170 million (that's $24 million per year, folks, the same as the Mariners' contract) - was somehow "disrespectful" to him. Due to that "disrespect" he opted to go to the Mariners, a team with even less playoff aspirations than the current, moribund Bronx-based franchise.

Many questioned Cano's use of the term "disrespect," and this author, among others, welcomed the opportunity for someone to disrespect us to the tune of $170 million. Or even $17 million.

Quite frankly, a client can utterly disrespect me and offer me only $1.7 million, or only one percent of the Yankees' clearly (cough) insulting offer. Try me. I will likely accept.

This past week, another New York (well, really New Jersey) athlete invoked the "disrespect" card as he packed up and headed to the West Coast. Giants' defensive lineman Justin Tuck and his two Super Bowl rings are heading to Oakland, where he will try to convince others to join him as he hopes to lead the hapless Raiders back to the playoff position that they occupied so often when John Madden prowled the sidelines as their coach. Tuck will be paid $11 million to play in Oakland for the next two years, and has lamented that the Giants did not try harder to retain his services.

BLOGGIN' BASEBALL II (FROM THE BLEACHERS) - ANDREW WOLFENSON

Today's *Newark Star-Ledger* contains an article about Tuck, and is headlined as follows: *Tuck rolls with punch, embracing fresh start, but feeling 'disrespected.'*

The article goes on to reveal that the Giants had offered Tuck a two-year contract for $6 million. He then went back to the team after he received his offer from Oakland, hoping for a counter-offer that did not materialize. According to the article, Tuck "probably would've taken a two-year, $8-million deal had it been offered." Apparently the Giants' failure to come up with the additional two million is what leaves Tuck feeling the "d" word.

Again, however, a little reality check is in order. Justin Tuck is 30 years old, which, to his chagrin, is considered "old" by NFL standards. Also, aside from a sparking three-game stretch last year, he was virtually invisible on the football field in 2013. The Giants again missed the playoffs completely. Tuck's main concern should have been helping the team put the best array of players on the field, so that he could help the G-Men return to gridiron dominance. Would a million dollars a year have made that much to him? He has his football salary and no doubt millions of dollars in endorsement money (Subway, Nike, etc). The extra million would not, in reality, mean that much to him.

Yet, he will be wearing the silver and black this season - because he felt disrespected.

Interestingly, the Lakers' Steve Nash, an all-time great who has missed all but ten games this season due to injury, made waves this week by disclosing that he intended to return to the NBA next year – because he wants the money. Media and public scorn followed, because, apparently, Nash should have said that he wanted to come back to help the Lakers, or to come back for the fans – but he was wrong in saying that it was about the money. What these people fail to realize, however, is that Nash's statement actually showed the fans and media proper respect – by being honest with them.

BLOGGIN' BASEBALL II (FROM THE BLEACHERS) - ANDREW WOLFENSON

Kudos to Steve Nash for telling the truth, especially because he said what is so manifest in professional sports today – that so many players change teams, or continue to play past their prime, just for the money.

As for Mr. Tuck, I will miss seeing you wearing the Giants' blue, much like I will miss seeing Robinson Cano in Yankee pinstripes – but I don't buy your whining about being disrespected. You and many other professional athletes are already paid way too much to play the game, especially in this economy and when so many people, this writer included, are working far more hours than in past years and, somehow, inexplicably, for less money. Walk a mile in my shoes. Take the verbal assaults that I endure on a daily basis from frustrated (often without reason) clients, annoying adversaries, and others. Take the daily stress inherent in my job (or that of so many others). Take the stress that so many have – of whether or not they will be able to make their next mortgage or rent payment, or keep the lights on, or feed their families. And take it all for a mere fraction of what you would have been paid by the Giants or Yankees.

Then come and talk to me about disrespect.

Overtime: Tuck's presence in the locker room was certainly missed, and it could be argued that his presence on the field has also been missed by a Giants' team devoid of an effective pass rush until the recent return of Jason Pierre-Paul. The reality on the field, however, is that Tuck is past his prime. He registered only five sacks in 2014, and played only five games in 2015, tallying one lone sack, before being sidelined for the remainder of the season with a torn pectoral muscle.

And while the Yankees certainly could have used Cano's bat in the team's lineup the past couple of seasons, his production while in Seattle (he has averaged 18 home runs, 80 RBI, and a .300 batting average) has been below his averages while in pinstripes and, arguably, not sufficient statistics to have merited the ten year, $240 million contract that he and his agent were demanding.

BLOGGIN' BASEBALL II (FROM THE BLEACHERS) - ANDREW WOLFENSON

NFL Star Aldon Smith's Bomb Threat at LAX; Is There a Bomb?

(Originally posted April 14, 2014)

Or maybe, he wasn't bluffing.

Yesterday, San Francisco 49ers linebacker Aldon Smith was arrested for telling TSA agents that he was carrying a bomb with him as he tried to get through security at LAX. Smith now faces up to a year in prison for making a false bomb threat at an airport. This is just the latest in a string of legally-related issues for Mr. Smith, including a suspected DUI, time spent in rehab (and suspension from the NFL) for alcohol and/or drug-related issues, and pending felony gun charges arising out of a 2012 incident in which illegal assault weapons were allegedly fired.

The NFL has had more than its share of run-ins with the law lately, and the character of its players has never been called into question like it has over the past twelve months. Former Patriots' tight end Aaron Hernandez still sits in prison, accused of murder, with issues surrounding how the New England brass could have missed the "red flags" of his past acting, presumably, as a warning sign to other teams to check the backgrounds of its players. Likely as a result of the Hernandez situation, Philadelphia recently severed ties with last year's leading receiver, DeSean Jackson, the same day that rumors of his gang-related involvement were reported upon in local papers. Jackson quickly signed with Washington, a team not immune to scandal, but Jackson's release presumably was done to point out that the Eagles did not want a Hernandez-type situation in their locker room.

The Eagles also said farewell to convicted dog-killer Michael Vick, who was then signed, inexplicably, by the New York Jets. The Jets' continued media circus and anti-Vick sentiment from the fans has already begun in earnest, so it should be an interesting season in the Meadowlands.

Back to Smith. He is a ferocious pass rusher and one of the best defensive players in the NFL. In 2012, the year that ended with team winning the Super Bowl, he recorded 19.5 sacks to lead the team (in fact, the most for one season in team history) and last year was able to record eight sacks despite missing five games to suspension. But as we have seen in the past, such ferocity on the field is sometimes matched by ferocity and recklessness off the field – witness Lawrence Taylor, the greatest linebacker in NFL history, for example, who has had more than his share of drug-related and legal troubles both during and after his playing career.

The police blotter has been rife with entries from the NFL over the past year, and several have dealt with the 49ers. Smith's teammate, quarterback Colin Kaepernick, was accused by a woman of improper sexual conduct with two other players - another member of the Niners and a member of the Seahawks. That investigation is pending. Last month, another member of the team's defense, Chris Culliver, was arrested on suspicion of felony hit and run after allegedly striking a bicyclist with his vehicle. The list, sadly, goes on and on.

Smith, however, appears to be a special case, a repeat offender, if you will. Suspension and rehab last year clearly did not leave a sufficient mark on Aldon to prevent the incident at the airport; in fact, any logical person knows that you cannot even joke about carrying a bomb when in an airport, so it is possible that this latest chapter in the Aldon Smith saga was nothing more than a cry for help, a cry that both the NFL and the San Francisco 49ers must take quite seriously.

Maybe Smith was not carrying a bomb in LAX yesterday, but instead, he, himself, is the bomb. Perhaps Smith realizes that he is combustible, and that, at any moment, he is going to "explode." The warning signs are all there. It is up to the league and the team to help this young man through his problems, and to take appropriate steps to see that both he and his fellow players are taken care of – both through protecting them from concussions/traumatic brain injuries and otherwise.

Tick … tick … tick.

Overtime: The charges were eventually dropped by the LA City Attorney after various interviews revealed that Smith never clearly stated that he had a bomb. He missed nine games that season due to suspension.

Tick … tick … tick …

A year later, however, on August 6, 2015, Mr. Smith was again arrested, this time in Santa Clara, for an alleged hit and run accident while driving under the influence. The following day, the 49ers released him from his contract. He signed with the cross-town Oakland Raiders, and for a while stayed on the right side of the law during his time in silver and black, until –

Tick … tick … tick …

BOOM!

On November 17, 2015, Smith was suspended for one year for violating the league's substance abuse policy.

Donald Sterling and the Hypocrisy of Both the NBA and NAACP

(Originally posted April 29, 2014)

At 2:00 this afternoon, NBA Commissioner Adam Silver will announce what will likely be fines and/or suspension against LA Clippers' owner Donald Sterling, the result of his racial and bigoted comments as recorded by his ex-girlfriend. The league is under great pressure to take action against Sterling – based not only on this most recent round of comments but also, as it is being argued, on his past history of racial insensitivity and bigotry.

Clearly, action must be taken against him. His comments against African-Americans, assuming that they were made and not doctored by a bitter ex-concubine, are horrific and cannot be condoned. As is usually the case, however, what we are seeing and hearing does not tell the full story.

The NBA should have known that Sterling was a bigot, the masses argue, based on past comments made by him, deposition transcripts, and a record $2.7 million dollar verdict against him (he is a well-known Los Angeles slumlord) in the past for discriminating against potential African-American, Hispanic, and single mother tenants. This was all public knowledge, his critics charge, and that the league should not have let it gone on for so long.

Michael Jordan apparently stated that in a league dominated by African-Americans, this type of conduct could not be permitted. He was half-right. The number of African-Americans playing basketball does not alter the hatred conveyed in his statements, or the racial intolerance that cannot be present. But - even if Sterling had been the owner of a National Hockey League franchise (or another league with a slight minority presence), such statements could not pass without ramifications.

Today, the masses may get their wishes, to a certain degree. Today, the Donald Sterling era in Los Angeles will take a turn, but not as dramatic a turn as some desire. The likelihood is that he will be fined and suspended, but the Commissioner's Office cannot force him to sell the team. The other owners can pressure him to do so, but it remains to be seen whether that will happen. Thus far, the only owners who have spoken out against Sterling are African-American, like Jordan. There has been a deafening silence from the white ownership bloc.

Will the owners try to get him to sell? Perhaps – but likely not for the reason that is desired by the masses. Already various companies have pulled their endorsement deals from the Clippers. Less revenue for any team means a loss for all teams. And if the fans stop going to the games in order to protest the owner's statements, then, similarly, a smaller gate purse means less money in the hands of the other/visiting team. Any action taken against Sterling will not likely be borne of racial indignation, therefore, but rather of concern for their own wallets.

*****

At the same time, the venom being spewed against the NBA has not, inexplicably, also been aimed at the NAACP. In 2009, the National Association for the Advancement of Colored People gave a lifetime achievement award to Donald Sterling. Before the most recent tape of Sterling's bigotry and vitriol was released, they were poised to present him with his second lifetime achievement award. So why don't the standards being applied to the NBA also apply to the NAACP?

If in fact his positions were "common" or "public knowledge," such that the NBA should have taken action against Sterling in the past, then how can the NAACP justify awarding this bigot a lifetime achievement award? Better yet, two lifetime achievement awards?

The NAACP brain trust no doubt was aware of the discrimination allegations and verdict against Donald Sterling. Any information that was or should have been possessed by the NBA should also have been known by the NAACP. So why would the NAACP honor this man? Why honor this man, who possesses such hatred toward their intended beneficiaries?

One reason – donations. Even though it appears certain that Sterling has no love for African-Americans, he has been a big donor to the NAACP. As a result, the NAACP bestowed him with what must be one of its top honors, and it had intended to do it again until the most recent tapes were released.

And tonight, the NAACP is apparently planning a protest outside of the Clippers-Warriors playoff game. I have not heard, however, about any plans for them to return Sterling's donations to him.

*****

Sterling will be made to pay for his comments. His wallet will be dented, and he may be pressured to sell his basketball team. His second NAACP lifetime award has been withdrawn. The NBA brass will say all of the right things about racial tolerance and the need to eradicate hatred and bigotry from its ranks, and the NAACP will point to Sterling as an example of hatred and bigotry that must be eliminated from society at large. The NBA, however, will no doubt be protecting its own financial interests and, to a lesser extent, trying to promote racial harmony. And the NAACP? Any protest should ring hollow, in light of its past history of feting Sterling because of his donations, which apparently outweighed the very public knowledge of his bigotry.

The Donald Sterling story is not simply "black and white" with respect to its facts and undercurrents, nor is it even a story of "white" and "black" with respect to color. It is, with respect to its main parties, a story of green. And, as is too often the case, it is no doubt a story of hypocrisy.

Overtime: **Sterling was forced to sell the team, which sale was approved by the League following legal action. The other issues at play here, as noted in**

the original post, however, still merit further discussion. The head of the local NAACP chapter stepped down from his position, but it does not seem that much investigation was performed into why the organization would have taken money from and/or honored a man who was apparently well-known as a racist. At the same time, the coach and players who acted so defiantly against Sterling when the latest comment made news were never called to answer why they had ignored the otherwise public facts about him when they were signing their multi-million dollar contracts. That still does not make any sense.

Michael Sam - Don't Call Me a Gay Player - Wait, Please Do

(Originally posted May 15, 2014)

"I just wish you guys would just see me as Michael Sam the football player instead of Michael Sam the gay football player."

Well, maybe not.

It is being reported that the OWN Network will be airing a "docu-series" on Michael Sam and his attempts to become the first openly-gay player in the National Football League. Not surprisingly, this announcement has drawn mixed reactions. On this morning's ESPN "Mike and Mike" radio show, for example, host Mike Greenberg hailed the announcement, likening Sam's presence to Jackie Robinson as baseball's first African-American player and opining that if the current technology had been in place back in 1947, no doubt Robinson's efforts would have been similarly documented and followed.

Co-host Mike Golic, however, offered a differing opinion, one which better sums up the various issues at play with Sam. Golic completely agreed with the network's decision to create and air the show, he said, because it will be a ratings bonanza. He questioned why Sam would agree to do the show, however, both in light of the above comment and because, as he explained, Sam's sole focus must be on making the Rams' roster for 2014. The distraction of a television show, no doubt, will detract from this focus.

Sam was drafted in the seventh round of the recent NFL draft. According to experts, he was drafted so low not because of his sexual orientation or the distraction that his presence would cause, as some have opined, but because he may be too small to play his chosen position in the NFL. Being an excellent college player (he was the SEC's Defensive Player of the Year) does not always translate into a stellar pro career, as a road littered with former Heisman Trophy winners who never succeeded in the NFL serves to prove. Sam is not guaranteed a roster spot when the team begins the 2014 season. All but one of the players similarly drafted (in the seventh round) in 2013 are, in fact, still in the NFL (whether on the active roster or practice roster) so the odds are in his favor, but his roster spot is not assured.

Why he would invite the additional distractions of more camera crews, therefore, must be questioned. One must assume that he will be subject not only to the additional glare of the cameras, but that he will be sitting down for nightly discussions with the series' producers to offer his thoughts on training camp and his progress. These discussions will, naturally, pull him away from team activities and/or his required time at reviewing the team's playbook, etc. And if he does not perform to the best of his abilities, he will put the Rams in a difficult position; if the team does not retain him, they will be opening themselves up to unnecessary scrutiny from those who will opine that he was released because of his sexual orientation or the media circus that accompanied his presence.

And what of his teammates? Surely the Rams' brass knew that they would be inviting increased media coverage by drafting Sam, much like the Cleveland Browns' ownership knew of the media storm that would follow them when they drafted media darling Johnny Manziel. For Sam to interject an increased layer of media through his own reality television show, however, is likely something that the team leaders did not anticipate – and with which it cannot be pleased. The team cannot, however, deny Sam his desired show, for fear of media backlash. Sam's teammates certainly did not sign on for the increased glare, and one must wonder if, there is an additional intrusion from the television show, how that may affect other players and/or their abilities to make the final roster.

Meanwhile, to think that Sam's "experience" in trying to make the team will be "realistic" is likely nothing more than folly. How other players and coaches interact with Sam will likely be sanitized, with the others fearing retribution if they step out of line. We learned last year of the macho attitude that still pervades certain locker rooms, when Miami's Jonathan Martin left the team after being subject to abuse by teammates Richie Incognito and others. Somewhere, next month, a seventh-round draft pick will be burned on the playing field by a potential teammate. Others will call out the draftee, calling him names which may include slurs like "faggot," "pussy," and other words which have been used to demean one's manhood for years. But not in St. Louis – the other players will no doubt be extremely careful not to use any derogatory or demeaning terms toward Sam, for fear of being exposed as a homophobe or bigot if they use such words in dealing with Michael Sam. The baptism of Michael Sam into the NFL, I would urge, will be much different than those who came before him. Not that there's anything wrong with that, but it likely won't make for stellar television.

Will it be worth it for OWN to broadcast what will essentially be a cleaned-up version of HBO's "Hard Knocks?" Absolutely. People will watch, and advertisers will buy commercial time during its airings.

Will it be worth it for Sam? That is yet to be seen. No doubt he is being paid for the show, so he will benefit in that way. Also, he may view himself as an activist, and said yesterday that "if seeing my story helps somebody else accept who they are and to go for their dreams too, that's great." But Michael Sam the draftee can only do so much, especially if he never has an NFL career. Michael Sam, the NFL player, or Michael Sam, starting linebacker for the St. Louis Rams, can do so much more. As Mike Golic said, Sam should be focusing all of his energies on making the team.

The TV crews will wait. The telling of his life story can wait.

He should be focusing on making himself the best player he can be, for the longer his career lasts, the longer his message will resonate.

Overtime: Unfortunately, any positive message that Sam could have delivered has been obscured by his performance (actually, lack of

performance) on the field. He was cut by the Rams, and then signed by the Cowboys to their practice squad. He never made their actual roster, however, and eventually caught on with the Montreal Alouettes of the Canadian Football League for the 2015 season. A few weeks after he signed with Montreal, he was granted permission to leave the team for what was described as "personal reasons" and was placed on the suspended list. He returned to the team later that month, and eventually saw action in the team's sixth game. He missed the next game with what was reported to be a sore back, and then left the team one day later – citing concerns with his mental health – and was again placed on the suspended list.

He has not returned to the team, nor has he signed with another professional football team. He has stated publicly that he believes his decision to come out prior to the draft has had an adverse affect on his playing career. In this writer's opinion, comments like that completely undermine the positive message that he originally set out to convey. This is sad for Sam, as well as for any other homosexual players who now have even more reason to keep their sexual orientation a secret.

Baseball, Football, and Differing Views on Domestic Violence

(Originally posted July 24, 2014)

Last night, former major league baseball player Chuck Knoblauch was arrested and charged with allegedly assaulting his ex-wife. Knoblauch, a four-time All-Star who spent the majority of his twelve-year professional career with the Minnesota Twins and New York Yankees, retired following the 2002 season. Six times he scored more than 100 runs in a season, ten times he stole more than 25 bases in a season, and earned several pieces of hardware: he was the 1991 Rookie of the Year, won the "silver slugger" award as the best hitting second baseman in 1995 and 1997, and also captured the "gold glove" in 1997 as the best-fielding second baseman.

Lately, however, it appears as if his desire for "hitting" has taken a new form. In 2010, he was convicted of hitting his first wife and sentenced to a year of probation. Now, he is accused of assaulting his latest wife, from whom he was divorced in 2012.

Reaction from the Minnesota Twins organization was swift. Knoblauch had been slated to be inducted into the team's Hall of Fame, and was to be honored with an on-field celebration on August 23. His induction, however, has been canceled – based, according to the team statement issued today, "in light of recent news reports."

On the same day that Knoblauch's entry into Minnesota baseball immortality was derailed by his off-the-field actions, the National Football League announced that Baltimore Ravens (and former Rutgers University) running back Ray Rice had been suspended for two games this upcoming season following a February incident in an Atlantic City casino whereby he allegedly knocked his then-fiancée (now wife) cold while the two rode an elevator. He had been indicted by a grand jury in Atlantic County of third-degree assault, and, rather than proceed to trial, he entered the court's Pre-Trial Intervention program. Under that program, there is no plea of guilty or innocent – instead, he was placed on a probation-type program, and as long as he stays clean and complies with the court's requirements for a specified period of time, the charge will be dismissed.

Clearly, the "punishment" meted out by the Twins seems much more severe than that handed down by the NFL. Barring Knoblauch from the team's Hall of Fame is as harsh a measure as the Twins could take – granted, it was not the first time that he has been accused of such conduct, but it is admirable that the team took a moral high ground and reacted in this manner. On the other hand, the mini-suspension handed down by the NFL, which is only half as long as the suspension that he would have received had he tested positive for marijuana, is quite the opposite, the proverbial "slap on the wrist."

Some may argue that two games is sufficient because Rice was never convicted of the assault, nor did he plead guilty. The suspension, they could argue, is based on a hypothetical - what Rice may or may not have done, not what he was actually proven to have done. To those, however, I would urge that he also was not acquitted, nor were the charges dropped for lack of evidence. His entry into the Pre-Trial Intervention program eliminated any chance of this argument being relevant – and clearly the NFL believes him to be guilty – so why not send a real message that conduct of this type truly would not be tolerated? A letter written by Commissioner Roger Goodell to Rice after the suspension was levied spoke of "integrity" and "confidence of the public," and referred to a lack of tolerance for domestic violence.

A mere two-game suspension, however, does not accomplish the league's stated purpose. Perhaps furthering the common perception of football being a game for "tougher" players than baseball, today's remedial actions, when juxtaposed against each other, reveal that those at the baseball management level are far more serious in reining in overly-done displays of testosterone when it comes to domestic violence than are their gridiron counterparts.

Extra Innings/Overtime: Any news reports regarding Knoblauch died down quickly, if for no other reason than it seemed that nobody cared. Perhaps this was because the news was so overshadowed by the Rice affair. Commissioner Goodell took tremendous heat for what was perceived to be a "light suspension" for Rice, especially after video surfaced showing the actual knockdown. Rice claimed that he and his then-fiance (now wife) had been forthright and open with the Commissioner regarding the events in the elevator that evening. Goodell disagreed, and banned Rice from the NFL – based largely, no doubt on the public outcry and the high level of embarrassment heaped upon the NFL when the video was made public. Eventually the suspension was reduced, but Rice has yet to put on an NFL uniform since he was initially suspended. The NFL now has more concrete procedures in place regarding the penalties to be handed out to players suspected of or convicted of domestic violence.

Domestic Violence Forces Drug Use to Sports' Back Seat

(Originally posted September 14, 2014)

It appears that the issue of performance-enhancing drug usage in professional sports such as baseball and football has, to a certain extent, run its course. Its "time in the spotlight" has faded, replaced by more salacious issues, and while the governing powers will continue to presumably test for such PEDs and levy penalties based on same, the level of outrage that had, up until very recently, accompanied such usage and suspensions has abated.

Two days ago, slugger Chris Davis of the Orioles was handed a 25-game suspension for testing positive for amphetamines – as there are only 17 games left in the regular season, this means that Baltimore (currently in first place in their division) will be without its powerful first baseman for at least the first eight games of the playoffs, should they advance that far into the post-season. The suspension of a playoff-bound team's major contributor so late in the season, and a suspension which would easily derail the team's World Series aspirations, would usually be cause for screaming headlines – but in a sports world dominated by stories of domestic violence and alleged child abuse, the story barely merited an entire article unto itself, buried within the sports pages of my local paper.

It appears that Davis, who steadfastly denies ever using PEDs, had taken Aderall without proper permission from the league. Aderall – often used to treat ADHD – can be approved for use by a player through what is termed a "Therapeutic Use Exemption" – and apparently Davis had such an exemption in 2013 (and possible before) but not for this season. 119 such exemptions were given, according to posted reports, in 2013. The use of such TUE's was also referenced with respect to Alex Rodriguez, who apparently had such exemptions often in the past, including his 2009 MVP season while with the Yankees.

239

The first positive test for this stimulant, which is known as a performance enhancer (and which may explain the large number of major leaguers – 119?? - who presumably suffer from ADHD), simply leads to additional testing. Suspension is only warranted after the second positive test – which means that Davis must have tested positive at least once in the past.

Why would a player who has already tested positive risk a second positive test and suspension? As I have pointed out previously, the answer boils down to money. A look at Davis' career and earnings proves this point: Over his first two seasons in the league, with the Texas Rangers, Davis slugged 38 home runs. During the next four seasons, he played in only 163 games, the equivalent of a full season, and hit but 11 home runs. 2012 brought a surge to 33 home runs, and that was followed up with a monster 2013 campaign during which he led the league and set a new Orioles' team record with 53 homers. Through 127 games this season, he has 26 homers.

So we again pose the question as to why he, or anyone, would use PEDs to increase his statistics other than the sheer glory of same? The answer remains $$$. Davis played in only part of four seasons from 2008 through 2011. In 2012, when he hit 33 home runs, he earned $488,000. Based on that home run total, his salary increased seven-fold to $3,300,000 in 2013. And then, after his 53-homer explosion last year, his salary tripled to $10,350,000. Over the past two years, therefore, his salary has increased by $9,862,000 per year – or, to put it in different terms, his current annual salary is 21 times greater than it was only two years ago. *If someone offered me such an incredible salary increase and financial stability over such a short period of time with the only possible ramification being what amounts to a one-month suspension from my job, then I, without question, would also take Aderall. Anyone would do the same.*

So where is the outrage? I haven't seen it.

Similarly, it was reported on Thursday that Indianapolis Colts' defensive lineman Robert Mathis would miss the remainder of this season due to a torn Achilles' tendon. The blurb in the newspaper about the injury, however, also stated, matter-of-factly, that Mathis had, less than two weeks ago, started serving a four-game suspension for violating the NFL's performance-enhancing drug policy. That same blurb also noted that Mathis set a team record last season with 19 ½ quarterback sacks, which also led the NFL. No connection, however, was drawn between his usage of the PED's and his record-setting performance. He claims that he was taking some form of fertility drug. The NFL has not confirmed.

At the same time, the NFL and its players' association are negotiating changes to the NFL's drug policy – to lighten the suspensions – and eliminate for some positive tests. Denver wide receiver Wes Welker is serving a suspension for violating the league's drug policy. He claims that someone slipped something into his drink at the Kentucky Derby. If the changes are approved by the league and players' association, he (and others) will be eligible for immediate reinstatement.

The use of such PEDs continues, it appears, and lightening the penalties will, to a certain extent, simply validate the use of same. The NFL, of course, now is facing much larger problems than players who use drugs to increase their performance. The past couple of weeks have proven embarrassing to the league with respect to actions taken off the gridiron – and although all of the people who have been accused and/or convicted of abuse took those actions independently of their stature as NFL players, the actions resonate to the field as well.

The Ray Rice domestic abuse situation took a dramatic toll last week when TMZ released a video showing Rice knocking out his then-fiancé with one punch. Incredibly, his initial suspension for the charge had been two games. Now, in anticipation of the public response to the video, the Baltimore Ravens terminated his contract and the NFL has suspended him indefinitely. The Commissioner's Office is under attack for its initial mishandling of the allegations against Rice, and questions abound as to whether or not the league was in possession of the damning video before its release by TMZ.

Meanwhile, it has just been announced that the Carolina Panthers have finally taken the step of deactivating Greg Hardy for today's game – Hardy has been convicted of domestic assault by a judge and is awaiting re-trial on appeal. Ray McDonald, meanwhile, will be taking the field for the San Francisco 49ers, despite the fact that he was recently arrested for domestic violence.

On the other hand, the Minnesota Vikings head into today's action without All-Pro running back Adrian Peterson, who has been indicted on child abuse charges. The allegations against Peterson, that he beat his four-year old son with a branch, or a "switch", are even more horrific when one considers the fact that another child of his died at the hands of an abuser less than a year ago.

We live in a world of news cycles. A story breaks, is reported on incessantly, and is then replaced with a new, more salacious story. This appears to be the case with PEDs – the question is whether the leagues are focusing so much on outside issues, such as domestic violence, that it must turn away from the fight against drugs for the moment, or whether the realities of drug use, especially PED's, are merely being accepted by the leagues. Just this week, *Sports Illustrated* re-posted a 2004 article about PED's in baseball – and which focused primarily on former MVP and admitted PED user Ken Caminiti. Back then, the article declared, PED use was rampant throughout major league clubhouses. Is it really feasible to assume that things are different now?

Extra Innings/Overtime: The Domestic Violence issue has played out in a very interesting way in the NFL. Ray Rice's suspension was later changed to a year, but even after the suspension ended he has still not found a team for re-entry into the league. On the other hand, Greg Hardy, who can only be described as a repeat offender as new allegations surfaced regarding his activities, found a new home with Dallas, a team seemingly hell-bent on becoming an island for lost souls in the NFL. Hardy's term with the Cowboys

can best be described as tumultuous, with many calling for him to be cut from the roster and the team having had to intervene in order to have him remove offensive twitter comments and to perform spin control on comments made to the media.

The fact that Hardy has been given a second chance and that Rice has not, however, may be due to the different positions that the men play. Skilled defensive players will always find work in the NFL, much like left-handed relief specialists will always be welcome on a major league baseball roster. At the same time, the role of the running back has diminished to the point where rushers, even great rushers, have a short shelf life and are almost completely fungible. Today's star runner is, for the most part, tomorrow's has-been, replaced by a younger, faster back who can also fit into a team's offensive scheme. Now if Rice had been an All-Pro quarterback, like the person in the next post, no doubt he would be playing today.

Belichick Can't Be Solely to Blame for Inflation Scandal

(Originally posted January 22, 2015)

"Deflategate" has become the latest entrant into our collective sports vocabulary, as the NFL office is investigating allegations that the New England Patriots improperly used overly-deflated footballs during last week's romp over the Indianapolis Colts. The allegations have cast a dark shadow over what is supposed to be a two-week lovefest leading up to the Super Bowl, and comes at a time when the NFL brass was no doubt hoping to put aside one of its most difficult seasons, a year memorable not for accomplishments on the field, but rather for the multiple incidents of abuse off of the gridiron. Many have called for sanctions against not only the team, but its robotic, Darth Vader-like coach, Bill Belichick. In a classic "good v. evil" scenario, however, there have been few, if any calls, for penalties to be levied against the man who, almost unquestionably, was his accomplice should the allegations regarding this dastardly deed prove to be true.

*****

Many years ago, before he became a member of the World Champion New York Knicks and long before he was a United States Senator from New Jersey, Bill Bradley was a star basketball player at Princeton University. Legend has it that the man known as "Dollar Bill" was practicing free throw shots before a game one day and complained to officials that the rim was not in the right place – the rim was examined and, voila!, it was a quarter-inch too far to one side.

Is this story true? Legend says that it is. Whether or not it is true, however, it stands for the proposition that the true greats know their equipment, and that any variation, no matter how slight, will make a difference in their game.

245

BLOGGIN' BASEBALL II (FROM THE BLEACHERS) - ANDREW WOLFENSON

Tom Brady was a sixth-round draft choice from the School up North. He has been the quarterback for the entirety of the Patriots' dynastic run under Coach Belichick, winning three Super Bowls and participating in two others that ended in defeat at the hands of Eli Manning and the New York football Giants. He is regarded as one of the best quarterbacks of his era, and has unquestionably stamped his ticket to football's Hall of Fame upon his retirement.

Tom Brady also has movie-star looks, and the most talked-about hair in the NFL since Jason Seehorn. He is married to a woman who has alternately modeled and played her part in creating some of the most genetically-perfect children to grace this planet, along with families like the Beckhams, the Jolie-Pitts, and the Wolfensons. He is not just a football star, but he is also a pop icon. He is the good to Bill Belichick's evil.

*****

One of the best athletes ever to play in New England was Ted Williams. It was said that Williams possessed the best eyesight of any batter ever to play professional baseball, and he claimed to be able to see the ball so well that he could say where his bat made contact with the ball. Legend has it that he was once put to the test, that they put shoe polish on his bat, had him take a few batting practice swings, and then asked him where the ball and bat made contact (on the laces, above laces, etc). As the story goes, he answered properly each time.

*****

If in fact eleven of the dozen balls used by the Patriots in last week's game were under-inflated, there is simply no way that Tom Brady did not realize that he was holding lighter footballs. It is also folly to assume that he did not gain an edge from using the lighter, flatter ball, or else there would have been no reason for the Patriots to alter the balls after they were examined by the referees (assuming, of course, that they were guilty of doing so – wink, wink).

When asked about the scandal on a radio show the other day, Brady laughed and said that he had not heard anything about it, and, of course, professed complete ignorance as to the possibility that the team had tampered with the game balls. Of course, the interviewer never asked the more probative question – whether he believed that the balls felt any different during the game. Surely a craftsman such as Brady, with over a decade of success on the field, would have made note of the fact that his one occupational tool was altered.

Brady, however, is a good guy. As such, nobody seems to be questioning his possible involvement in this scenario, other than former coach John Madden. Football expert Peter King, of mmqb.com, showed as such this morning on ESPN radio when he indicated that since Brady's record is pristine (he called him the "Derek Jeter of football"), he was not ready to accuse him of being involved – yet he believes that Belicheck, due to his prior transgressions (2007's "Spygate", etc), is likely culpable should any wrongdoing be found. And yes, as the Head Coach he should be held accountable for everything that goes on under his watch, much like Sean Payton, the Saints' Head Coach, was suspended for a year following the "Bountygate" scandal – even though the bounties were allegedly the brainchild of his Defensive Coordinator, and were not given out under his direction.

But Belicheck does not touch the balls during the game. He does not throw the passes, and he does not hand the ball off to the running backs.

Those are Brady's jobs. As such, he is the one person who could most benefit from altering the air pressure in the balls, and the one who would be in the best position to note if they were at an improper inflation level. I have long opined that reactions to the steroid scandal in baseball are based in part on whether the accused players are friendly (David Ortiz and Andy Pettitte) as opposed to surly and petulant (Barry Bonds, Roger Clemens, Mark McGwire) and it seems like the same "good v. evil" standards are being used here. It makes no sense to call for Belichick's head and, at the same time, not ask for Brady's handsome face on the same platter.

It is easy to jump on an anti-Belichick bandwagon. He is surly, mostly non-communicative, has been found guilty of cheating in the past and has been wildly successful as the Patriots' head coach. There have been, however, only three consistencies during the Patriots' run of Super Bowl and playoff successes – Bill Belicheck, Tom Brady, and, if you believe the stories, cheating. You cannot punish one without the other.

If it is found that the team used improper balls in order to advance their edge over an already overmatched Colts' team (no matter how light the balls were, a 45-7 romp was due to much more), then the team should be sanctioned – loss of draft picks, fines, etc. Its coach should be sanctioned – so Belicheck should be suspended for a game or more, and possibly fined. And yes, its quarterback, the likely accomplice, should also have his sterling reputation tarnished and face sanctions as well – because he knew.

He had to have known. And then, when he is penalized, he will not be laughing about it any more – or maybe he will be, because if he is suspended he will be able to watch the game in the comfort of his home, at his mansion, surrounded by his model wife and perfect children. It's good to be Tom Brady … especially when nobody questions your honor and you have the perfect foil as your sidekick.

Think about some of the greatest duos in history. Ruth and Gehrig. Abbott and Costello. Martin and Lewis. Laurel and Hardy. Bonnie and Clyde. And remember to add Belichick and Brady.

Overtime: Everyone knows what happened next. The NFL did an investigation and concluded something along the lines that there was impropriety with respect to the air pressure in the balls, and that Tom Brady maybe sorta coulda known something about it. Commissioner Roger Goodell, not wanting to seem like he was playing favorites with his friend (Patriots owner Robert Kraft) and still smarting from allegations that he was too soft on the multiple wife/girlfriend abusers amongst the NFL's players, took decisive action. The Patriots were hit with a fine and Tom Terrific was suspended for four games. Tom Teflon then sued the NFL and a Federal Court Judge ruled that the Commissioner's role as judge and jury was improper – hence the suspension was struck down. As of the publication of this book, the Patriots, with their fearless leader at Quarterback, have once again steamrolled through the NFL with an undefeated record. In fact, it can be argued the only thing more perfect than the Patriots' record is their quarterback. Clearly he can do no wrong, and no evil or difficulty will ever befall him.

THE END

ALSO BY ANDREW WOLFENSON

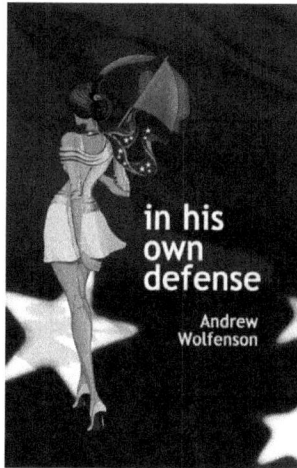

"*People may hate lawyers but they love to read about them and this book proves why.* **In His Own Defense** *is a realistic look at the human drama that surrounds a high-stakes criminal case. The pitch-perfect prose and provocative plot compel you to read on, late into the night. New Jersey's own Andy Wolfenson is a north-of-the-Mason-Dixon line answer to John Grisham.*" – Henry Klingeman, Esq., Criminal Defense attorney and former Assistant U.S. Attorney for the State of New Jersey.

What happens when an attorney is wrongfully accused of murdering a client's husband? Are conversations and interactions between the client and attorney protected by the Attorney-Client privilege, or is the attorney capable of defending himself against the false accusation, even if his actions prove damaging to the client?

Eric Goldberg is a New Jersey attorney who is first seduced, and then falsely accused of murder, by one of his clients. While testing the boundaries of the attorney-client privilege in conversations with the local police, he travels to Brazil to locate the one person who can clear his name. There, while the police from two countries search for him, he gains the assistance of a transplanted American architect and his free-spirited girlfriend, who lead him through the streets and clubs of Sao Paulo searching for his accuser.

In His Own Defense is available on Amazon.com and for Kindle

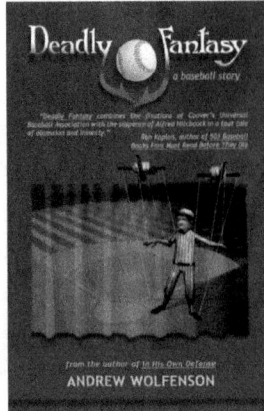

Deadly Fantasy: A Baseball Story

The perfect gift for fantasy baseball players and/or fiction lovers

"Who would ever think a game amongst friends would turn to deception and murder? ... Andrew Wolfenson takes loyalty and the American Pastime where they've never been before by playing Fantasy League Baseball with a life and death scoreboard, unquestionably making this book a home run." – Jon D'Amore, Author of the true mob story, The Boss *Always* Sits In the Back.

Over 33 million people in the United States participate in fantasy baseball and/or football leagues, and these leagues generate over two billion dollars per year in revenue. Some take their participation in such fantasy leagues more serious than others, suspending reality as they try to fulfill their dreams of serving as a major league owner or General Manager. For Jeff Goldstein, fantasy baseball is not just a game; participation in the league takes over his life. His obsession with winning his fantasy league, and its $150,000 prize, consumes his every thought and threatens his relationship with his girlfriend, his friends, and his job. How far will Jeff go in his desire to win the league? What actions will he take, or ask others to take, as he struggles to separate fantasy from reality?

Deadly Fantasy: A Baseball Story is available on Amazon.com and for Kindle.

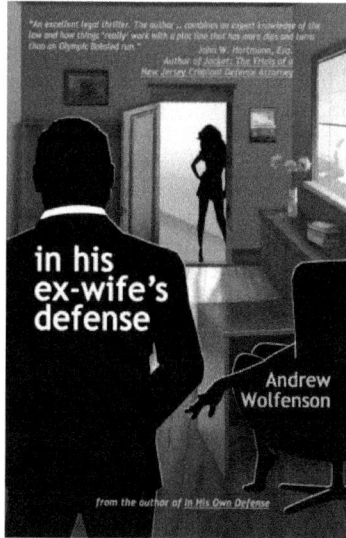

In His Ex-Wife's Defense

New Jersey attorney Eric Goldberg is back, and he's up to his neck in the most emotionally-challenging and potentially difficult case of his career. When his ex-wife is charged with vehicular homicide and turns to Eric for help, he is forced to not only battle the burden of representing the woman whose infidelity led to the end of their marriage, but also faces the daunting task of representing the first person to be locally prosecuted under a law regarding texting and driving.

Eric's varied emotions regarding his ex-wife and the stress of his internal conflict are further complicated when a former attorney trying to further his own political aspirations continuously publicizes the case, and by the fact that the Prosecutor handling the case is a very attractive young woman. At the same time, Eric is being pursued by a reporter who resembles a woman from his not-so-distant past. With all these distractions, will he be able to win the case for his ex-wife?

"In His Ex-Wife's Defense is an excellent legal thriller. The author hit the mark here. He combines an expert knowledge of the law and how things

"really" work with a plot line that has more dips and turns than an Olympic Bobsled run. As for the ending - guaranteed that you will not see it coming. This page turner is a must read!" - John W. Hartmann, Esq., Criminal Defense Attorney and Author of <u>Jacket: The Trials of a New Jersey Criminal Defense Attorney</u>

"A novel should educate and not misstate ... Andrew's books are refreshing because he does give the reader an accurate reflection of the legal system, right down to a realistic portrayal of the interaction between lawyer and client. I am impressed by his presentation and the ease with which he tells a story from start to finish." - John Paragano, Esq., Criminal Defense Attorney and former Municipal Court Judge (Union Township 1999-2005)

In His Ex-Wife's Defense *is available on Amazon.com and for Kindle.*

www.ingramcontent.com/pod-product-compliance
Lightning Source LLC
LaVergne TN
LVHW051227080426
835513LV00016B/1449